CHRYSANTHEMUMS

CHRYSANTHEMUMS

beautiful varieties for home and garden

NAOMI SLADE

photography by

GEORGIANNA LANE

Gibbs Smith

Contents

INTRODUCTION

As the days shorten and bright summer moves into mellow autumn, the palette of colors in the garden shifts towards caramel and gold. Yet, one iconic and sometimes controversial flower stands fast, burning still stronger as the darkness falls. Admired since antiquity, chrysanthemums are now back in style, and blessed with old-school glamour and lashings of vintage chic, their star is now firmly in the ascendant.

Chrysanthemums are complicated. They are cherished and loathed, familiar and arcane, straightforward and awkward in equal measure. While the flowers are often derided and shunned, they are also ubiquitous, and those who love them do so with a passion that is overwhelming.

Cultivated for thousands of years, chrysanthemums were first domesticated in ancient China before spreading to Korea and Japan, making the transition from useful herb to exhibition flower at an early point. Introduced to the west in the eighteenth century, their popularity led to the appearance of florists' societies focused on the exhibition and celebration of chrysanthemums, and this resilient and long-lasting bloom is now one of the most commercially important cut flowers in the world.

Given their history, it is strange that such a horticulturally established genus could be poorly regarded, but although we think we know them, closer investigation reveals that chrysanthemums are not actually that well understood. Over the centuries, commerce, horticulture and exhibition have followed divergent paths, resulting in a situation that is far from clear cut. A conversation, therefore, may stray to chrysanthemums, but with at least three different groups of individuals operating in different ways, it is hard to keep track of precisely what sort of chrysanthemum is being discussed.

To iron out the confusion, it is helpful to understand how the plant has acquired its several different identities, and this is related to the duration for which the plant has been cultivated, the purposes for which chrysanthemums have been bred, and even the order in which breeding programs have taken place. Over time, a division has also arisen between plants that are hardy and those that are not, while the involved system of rules that are applied to exhibition plants has contributed to perceived complexity.

Looking at chrysanthemums through the eyes of their specialists, it is apparent that the overlap between the fields of interest is not as great as might be imagined. The classification system used for exhibition flowers is largely ignored by commercial growers, for example, despite the plants behaving in a similar way. Those cultivating chrysanthemums as a hardy plant, meanwhile, are unfussed about applying rules to their herbaceous borders, and their horticultural principles will differ.

When it comes to the lowly status of the blooms, the tides of fashion are with us always, and the things that are appreciated and lauded evolve. The late Victorian era and first part of the twentieth century was a boom time for chrysanthemums but as the years wore on, they became "work flowers," the hobnail boot of floristry, rather than its dancing slipper; stalwarts of church arrangements and funeral wreaths. British nurseries declined as trade became globalized, and while clubs and societies have carried on growing and exhibiting, in the absence of new blood they too have gradually ebbed.

Yet the story is one of redemption. As the popularity of chrysanthemums waned, the flowers themselves have improved, with plant breeders working their magic to increase usability and keep up with trends and florists' demands. Classic, old-fashioned flowers are also currently in vogue and chrysanthemums are now following in the wake of dahlias as stars of social media and objects of botanical lust, inspiring a new generation of chrysanthemum lovers, florist–growers and aficionados of vintage style.

Taken as a varied and versatile group, rather than sprig by doughty sprig, chrysanthemums' renewed popularity should come as no real surprise. The flowers with spiralling petals or bold quills lend themselves to a glamorous bouquet, while perky buttons and decorative forms fit perfectly into a bridesmaid's posy. As potted plants, they are perfect for brightening up an autumn windowsill, and the small vase of varied, fascinating, honey-scented daisies, sitting on my desk, has helped enormously with writing inspiration.

In truth, I have always had a soft spot for chrysanthemums. They are the cheerful flowers of grandmother-era gardens; the plants that my favorite uncle would pick up on one of his nursery-based spending sprees. He would then tuck them into a corner and forget about them – but they would flower generously and long in their state of sprawling neglect, nonetheless. The cheap and cheerful bunches of supermarket chrysanthemums don't offend me either, but when it comes to show chrysanthemums, my feelings are less clear cut. I appreciate the skill that goes into growing plants for exhibition, but I struggle aesthetically with the stiffness and rigor of formal display. So it was with delight that I discovered that, when approached from the aesthetic perspective of floral art, these same flowers can be soft, relaxed and utterly delicious.

The name chrysanthemum comes from the ancient Greek words *chrysos* and *anthemon*, which translate as "gold" and "flower" respectively. Colloquial names range from "mums" in the US to "chrysanths" or "xanths" in the UK and "chryssies" in Australia, and although the plant is now highly commodified, chrysanthemums have considerable symbolic status.

A traditional funeral flower and All Saints' Day decoration in Europe, chrysanthemums are associated with Thanksgiving in the US. In Britain, they featured in the literary works of Oscar Wilde and DH Lawrence; they were a feature of musical theatre, in *The Mikado* and later *The White Chrysanthemum*, while the Arts and Crafts movement and designers like William Morris cemented the flower's wider popularity as a design icon.

In Asia, chrysanthemums are also associated with long life and good health, and through their connection with natural philosophy and

communion with nature, they became linked with the Double Ninth Festival, which is celebrated on the ninth day of the ninth month – an auspicious double yang number. Originating in China, the festival includes the mythic search for the elixir of youth in the form of the dew that gathers on the flowers and foliage. Parallels were drawn between the robust performance of the plant late in the season and a vigorous old age, so the festival is a day of honoring elderly relatives.

Introduced to Japan in the eighth century, chrysanthemums grew to be an important cultural symbol. Adopting the Double Ninth Festival, the Japanese emperor adopted the Double Ninth festival and devised new chrysanthemum-based rituals to increase longevity, gazing at the flowers while being anointed by dew-soaked blooms. The Supreme Order of the Chrysanthemum became the country's highest honor and in 1889 a stylized chrysanthemum was adopted as the Imperial crest, and used not just as an official seal, but as a military insignia that was stamped on weaponry.

In the west, the arrival of the chrysanthemum inspired new societies and shows; they were proposed by Victorian writer James Shirley Hibberd as an autumn cure-all, with the entirely serious suggestion that the golden flowers would lift the spirits of miserable Londoners, and during the summer of love in 1967, they became a symbol of peace.

Yet, the theme of simultaneous plaudits and brickbats was established early. Artists such as Monet, Tissot, Van Gogh and Mondrian revelled in chrysanthemums, but novelist H Rider Haggard forbade his gardener to grow competition blooms. The husband of influential garden writer Margery Fish, meanwhile, was so vexed by their gardener neglecting his duties to "stroke and fondle" the chrysanthemums, that he took a knife and "slashed off all those pampered darlings at ground level."

Although it is easy to see the family relationship between chrysanthemums and all the other daisies, this book focuses on the cultivated chrysanthemum alone. Even so, deliberate interbreeding over millennia means that variation in the cultivated part of the genus is very high, so doing it justice presents some challenges. Through frequent mutation and directed breeding, there is a constant influx of new varieties, and with cultivars that differ across continents, and are used in different ways, picking a definitive "best" is simply not possible.

This book is, therefore, not an encyclopedia. It sets out to lift the heart and delight the eye; to inspire, intrigue and whet the appetite. It aspires to turn heads and change minds – while still remaining manageable and interesting. And for those who would know more, particularly about the art of exhibition, other excellent resources exist.

When it comes to choosing flowers, however, the complexity and multi-faceted nature of chrysanthemums lead one towards a logical and rather philosophical conclusion: don't seek to understand all that a chrysanthemum is and can be, but know what it is that you yourself want.

With a renaissance now long overdue, chrysanthemums should be celebrated and welcomed back into the fold of fashion. We should rejoice in their diversity and appreciate their manifold glories: little else can be such a willing workhorse and also display quite such a glamorous alter ego. Cheerful and carefree, they are stalwarts of the autumn border. The plant presents sufficient twists of technique to keep the most avid specialist absorbed. Ultimately, this is not just a flower with vintage charm and a venerable pedigree, it is also one with exquisite refinement and a truly modern twist.

THE HISTORY
AND BOTANY OF
CHRYSANTHEMUMS

TRANSPORTED FROM THE RUGGED MOUNTAINS OF CHINA
TO THE IMPERIAL COURT OF JAPAN AND THEN ONWARDS ACROSS THE
WORLD, CHRYSANTHEMUMS ARE TIMELESS, SPECTACULAR AND EVOCATIVE.
ASSOCIATED WITH ETERNAL DEPARTURE AS WELL AS VITALITY AND
LONGEVITY, THIS MODEST, MAGNIFICENT FLOWER STANDS ASTRIDE THE
BOUNDARY BETWEEN LIFE AND DEATH, AND THROUGH THE MEDIUM OF
POETRY AND PHILOSOPHY IT EVEN CALLS INTO QUESTION WHAT IT MEANS
TO BE HUMAN. BOTANICALLY COMPLEX AND EVEN CONTENTIOUS, THIS IS A
PLANT OF DICHOTOMIES, YET IT ILLUMINATES OUR LIVES WITH WARMTH AND
BRIGHTNESS AT THE POINT WHERE DARKNESS FALLS AND WE NEED IT MOST.

Chrysanthemums are part of our everyday scenery; they are familiar from every smiling bouquet and a staple of supermarket buckets and garage courtyards; yet in concept, meaning and significance, they are also so much more.

This is a flower that has moved humankind for millennia, provoking passion and inspiring legend. They are the stars of our great-grandparents' autumn borders and cottage gardens; the darlings of the showman's bench, yet they are also remarkably poorly understood. It is a strange and almost inconceivable truth that the monstrous exhibition bloom, wrought by who knows what arcane rites, could be the same flower that is perceived as cheap and slightly dull, while, as pretty late-season daisies of yore, chrysanthemums have all but been forgotten.

But perhaps they are not truly forgotten, and it is more that they have suffered a sea-change. After all, with their long and fascinating history, chrysanthemums have risen to become one of the most commercially important cut flowers in the world, and they are now, finally, starting to make a comeback as a garden plant, too. While the tradition of competitive exhibition is awaiting an influx of fresh energy, the flowers that underpin it are increasingly being embraced. And, introduced to a new audience by small-scale florist–growers and online influencers excited by their potential, chrysanthemums are starting to develop a cult following.

Sitting within the extensive Asteraceae family, *Chrysanthemum* is a genus of flowering plants containing several dozen species and a number of hybrids. When first described by Linnaeus in 1753, the genus originally contained 14 species, but over the years it has been split and reorganized, so it is now hard to be precise about numbers. Once classified as part of *Chrysanthemum*, the genera *Tanacetum*, *Leucanthemum* and *Argyranthemum* are now separate; and while the horticultural and floristry varieties spent some decades categorized in the genus *Dendranthema*, they were restored as chrysanthemums in 1999.

As a genus, *Chrysanthemum* is widespread, extending from western Europe to east Asia. The species from which cultivated chrysanthemums arose, however, are mostly native to the far eastern end of this range. These include *Chrysanthemum indicum* – now considered the defining species of the genus – together with others such as *C. sinensis, C. zawadazkii* and hybrids such as *Chrysanthemum x morifolium*. These, plus others, have been extensively interbred to create the many thousands of modern cultivars available today.

Into cultivation

Despite having a large wild range, there is a hotspot of chrysanthemum species in China, and it was there that the native plants were first domesticated. Originally used as a culinary and medicinal herb, chrysanthemums are recorded in cultivation as early as the Shang Dynasty, around 1600–1046 BC, and soon developed ritual and symbolic significance due to their late-blooming qualities.

In the Book of Rites, a philosophical text compiled during the lengthy Zhou Dynasty and attributed to Confucius (551–479 BC), there is a reference to "The late autumn moon and the yellow flowers of the chrysanthemum." In another early text, the flowers are associated with a healing pool which gave them the reputation of being able to bestow long life and venerable age. A later reference is found in the fifth of the famous Twenty Poems on Drinking Wine by Tao Yuanming, or Tao Qian (AD 365–427), in which he describes plucking chrysanthemums at the eastern edge of his property, gazing out at the mountain and struggling to find words to express the meaning he feels. This has variously been interpreted as concerning the close and the distant, the humble and the magnificent, the ephemeral flowers and the vast permanence of the mountain, and the relationship of these things to human existence. Over time, the literary and philosophical significance of this late-blooming wonder saw it profoundly associated with the Double Ninth festival (see p.11), which carried forward the idea of chrysanthemums as bearers of the elixir of life and imbued them with the ability to ward off impending senescence.

Between the eighth and tenth centuries AD, the cultivated chrysanthemum was introduced to Korea and then to Japan by Chinese monks, who imported the associated rituals as well. Here, the still relatively simple flowers were further hybridized and interbred with local wild species, and as they became larger, more dramatic and more refined, they grew in reputation and symbolism. Gradually, cultural differences started to emerge, with a Chinese preference for a tight, neatly incurved flower while the Japanese favored exotic, reflexed blooms with spiralling spidery petals or cascading curls.

A tradition of display also developed at an early point. In Japan, it is thought that the first Imperial Chrysanthemum Show was held as early as AD 910, and chrysanthemum festivals and exhibitions remain popular to this day.

架橋

灑紫

Chrysanthemum cultivation in the west

In the past, wild-collected plants would frequently die in transit or through horticultural inexperience, and although chrysanthemums appeared in Dutch literature in the seventeenth century, none persisted until 1789 when French merchant, Captain Pierre Blancard, returned from the far east with three specimens of *Chrysanthemum morifolium*, one white, one purple and one violet.

Of these, Old Purple was the sole survivor. A semi-double form with incurved petals, it was large for the time and soon became a desirable flower in French horticultural circles, eventually making its way to Britain. There, it flourished under glass, and as gardeners became increasingly inspired and excited, further expeditions were mounted to China and the far east. In 1824, John Parks returned to his sponsors, the Horticultural Society of London (later to become the Royal Horticultural Society), with an array of new chrysanthemums, and by 1826 there were an estimated 50 named varieties in Britain.

In 1843 there was another leap forward when the Society sent Robert Fortune on a plant-hunting trip to China and he returned with the 'Chusan Daisy', an early form of Pompon chrysanthemum. Such was its success that he was sent out again, this time to Japan, returning with a treasure trove of large reflexed and curly blooms in a range of colors. These exotic creatures became known as Japanese chrysanthemums, as distinct from the crisply incurved and more limited color range of the Chinese chrysanthemums that preceded them. Both these names have to a certain extent persisted as a term of reference.

Breeding and development

By now, chrysanthemums were much sought after and as this new, fabulous and diverse group of flowers took the gardening world by storm, hot on its heels came a new wave of florists' societies, dedicated to the appreciation and celebration of *Chrysanthemum* at the highest level. Among these was the Stoke Newington Florists' Society for the Cultivation and Exhibition of Chrysanthemums, which was set up in 1846 and, after several iterations, became the National Chrysanthemum Society (NCS) in 1894.

Because the original chrysanthemum arrivals were half-hardy, the main focus until this point had been on greenhouse and exhibition varieties for cutting, and, since its launch, this has remained the priority of the National Chrysanthemum Society in Britain and of other, similar, organizations around the world.

Yet breeding was going on apace, with the aim of producing plants that were hardier and more early-flowering. Gradually, advances made in both France and Britain saw the arrival of plants that would flower outdoors in mid-autumn, and then from early autumn until the frosts came. As sailing ships criss-crossed the globe, these were introduced to the Americas and the antipodes, and the trend caught on. Soon, great rivalry developed between growers in the USA, Australia and Europe, with great trade in the best plants taking place, too.

During the first half of the twentieth century, chrysanthemums remained extremely popular and prodigious strides were made. New varieties proliferated at the hands of such famous names

as John Woolman and Halls of Heddon in the UK, followed later by Ted King in the US and Ron and Lynn Seaton in Australia.

Around this time, however, there arose fundamental changes in chrysanthemum cultivation that would have a lasting impact. Progress in the development of hardy garden chrysanthemums had been rapid, driving a wedge between these and the older, greenhouse forms, while the 1940s saw the introduction of All Year Round (AYR) production of cut flowers. So it is at this point that chrysanthemums diverge, conceptually and horticulturally, as an increasingly clear distinction arose between the interests and skills of exhibitors, commercial growers and amateur gardeners, and this has brought us to where we are today.

The rise of the hardy chrysanthemum

The creation of the palimpsest of hardy chrysanthemums for garden use was an uncoordinated but worldwide effort, and this hinged on hybridizing the existing greenhouse chrysanthemums that had been derived from species introduced from China and Japan, with the highly cold-tolerant species, *Chrysanthemum zawadazkii* subsp. *latilobum* and *C. zawadazkii* subsp. *sibiricum*.

Some of the earliest work on cold-hardy chrysanthemums was published by German nurseryman Karl Foerster in 1909 (see p.119). Although progress was derailed by the outbreak of World War One, the baton was taken up by others in the late 1920s and 1930s, producing hybrids that were to become widespread and highly influential.

In America, Scottish immigrant Alex Cummings used Korean-collected seed that was thought to be from the Arnold Arboretum, Massachusetts, to grow hardy mums, which he used as one parent in his breeding program. The resulting hybrids became known as Korean chrysanthemums, although it was later decided that the 'Korean' species was *C. zawadazkii* subsp. *sibiricum*. Some of these scented Korean chrysanthemums were patented in the US in 1945.

In Britain, meanwhile, Enfield-based Amos Perry acquired and trialled *C. zawadazkii* from several sources and had soon hybridized them with "Japanese" chrysanthemums to raise new, hardy cultivars such as 'Clara Curtis', which is still available. These cultivars were named Rubellums, due to the otherwise unrelated naming of a sport of *C. zawadazkii* as *C. rubellum*.

Another notable chrysanthemum stable was that of Dr Ezra Jacob Kraus and Dick Lehman in 1930s America, who produced the Mums from Minnesota™, which includes 'Ruby Mound' (see p.168).

Throughout the latter half of the twentieth century, a range of other breeders avidly crossed and re-crossed Rubellums, Koreans and all sorts of other chrysanthemums besides, and as a result the genetic makeup of most cultivated chrysanthemums is extremely complex.

Hardy garden chrysanthemums were eventually classified as section 21 by the British National Chrysanthemum Society in 2006. The Plant Heritage National Collection of hardy *Chrysanthemum* is held by Judy Barker in Hertfordshire, Dr Andrew and Helen Ward of Norwell Nurseries in Nottinghamshire and Hill Close Gardens Trust in Warwickshire. An additional collection of *Chrysanthemum* (Charms and Cascade) is held by Leeds City Council in Yorkshire.

Understanding chrysanthemums

As we have seen, chrysanthemums are diverse and varied. They are highly interbred and differ in terms of their hardiness, but whether they are bred for showing, for the garden, or explicitly for floristry purposes, they all make exemplary cut flowers.

Traditionally, part of the charm and value of chrysanthemums is that they flower as the days shorten. This makes the hardier varieties ideal for brightening up the border from late summer until midwinter, and as long as the temperature doesn't drop too low, they will often persist outdoors for months. With the protection of a greenhouse, their showy but more tender relatives, the exhibition chrysanthemums, will also continue to bloom, providing cut flowers over a similar period.

This photoperiodic response (see p.24), or the regulation of flowering according to day length, also means that by manipulating the plants' exposure to light, a continual stream of flowers can be produced. This is of commercial value as it irons out the peaks and troughs of seasonality.

As garden plants, chrysanthemums are either hardy or half-hardy and the flowers come in a range of forms, including singles, doubles, spiders, quills and spoons. The half-hardy types grown under glass for exhibition or floristry often have larger flowers than the hardy garden perennials, and these can be grown as a spray or disbudded. Hardy plants have small to medium-sized blooms, which are charming rather than ostentatious or dramatic. These are the logical choice for a mixed border.

With this in mind, the classification system for chrysanthemums (see pp.26–29) can seem bewildering, but it is important to remember that this has been designed specifically as a tool to help with exhibition. For the average gardener the important factor is the fundamental growability of the plant; what it looks like, when it flowers, and whether it will make it through the winter. Knowing this, you can get on with designing a border or container arrangement, and plan for a harvest of cut blooms if that is what is required.

Selecting the right variety is key. Large, late exhibition blooms are glamorous but tender divas that require care and a cozy glasshouse to thrive – but there are lots of others which are much easier to succeed with. Some are half-hardy or borderline hardy, but if you pander to their modest foibles, lifting them or insulating them, they will perform. The hardiest perennial cultivars, meanwhile, can be highly rewarding and flower gloriously in a sunny border with minimal maintenance.

Finally, there are the varieties sold as "pot mums." These are typically somewhat tender perennials grown as an annual, so while it may be technically possible to overwinter them, it is not a sure thing. That said, developments and breeding programs are ongoing, and with the appearance of hardier specimens that flower into the winter months, all that might be about to change.

PHOTOPERIODISM

Chrysanthemums are "short-day plants," which are stimulated to flower as the nights get longer. This is called a photoperiodic response, and while temperature, cultivar and number of leaves play a part, the key thing that influences blooming time is the way that chrysanthemums use red and far-red light, which is captured by the plants' phytochrome system.

The phytochrome molecule, known as P, is made up of a series of carbon rings, with the amino acid cysteine as a functional group. The molecule takes two forms: PR absorbs red light at a visible wavelength of 660nm and promotes flower formation; PFR absorbs far-red light at an invisible wavelength of 730nm, which permits vegetative growth but inhibits flower formation. The trigger for blooming is thought to be linked to the relative amount of each form of the chemical present in the cells.

When PR absorbs red light, it is converted to PFR. The longer the day, the more red light can be absorbed, therefore the more PFR will be present and the plant does not flower. During the night, in the absence of light, PFR reverts slowly to PR. So the longer the night and the shorter the day, the more PFR is removed and the more PR is available, which stimulates flowering.

In an interesting twist, this conversion can be speeded up and the phytochrome molecule made to flip between the two states, by exposing it to one sort of light or the other: when PFR is exposed to far-red light, it is rapidly converted back to PR. Interrupting the period of darkness with even a short burst of visible red light, meanwhile, means that the PFR that has so far gradually converted to PR, rapidly converts back to PFR – which then remains at too high a level for the plant to flower. This is why it is important to plant chrysanthemums where they are not lit by external lights, or even subject to flashes of light from passing cars.

As a result of this, commercial growers can manage the flowering period through a combination of excluding the light during the day and interrupting the period of darkness, which is the basis of the All Year Round cut chrysanthemum industry. The strength of the photoperiodic response can vary, however. Using hardy chrysanthemums as an example, 'Dixter Orange' and 'Esther' have a weak photoperiodic response and will flower while the days are still fairly long, while 'Mrs Jessie Cooper', 'Emperor of China' and 'Capel Manor' flower very late indeed, which adds considerably to their garden value.

Generalized phytochrome molecule

Anatomy of a chrysanthemum

Chrysanthemums are in the Asteraceae, or daisy family, which includes relatives such as lawn daisies and chicory, marigolds, dahlias, rudbeckias and zinnias, together with thistles and dandelions. These have a flower that looks like a single colorful bloom but which is actually an inflorescence, composed of many small flowers.

In its simplest form, the capitulum or flower head is made up of a cluster of florets that sits within a receptacle. Around the periphery are the ray florets, which are characterized by a showy petal, and at the center is a circular hub of disc florets, each one an individual, usually fertile, flower, carrying pollen and nectar.

Chrysanthemums are herbaceous perennials; roots anchor the plant and a crown of buds gives rise to a clump of flowering stems. The leaves are alternate, pinnatisect and divided to a greater or lesser extent; they range from dark green through fresh green to grayish in color, and can vary widely, depending on cultivar.

The scent, where it exists, is distinctive and the leaves of some plants give off a robust, spicy, lemony fragrance when crushed. In certain varieties the foliage also colors attractively in autumn. The plant often spreads via fleshy, rooted underground stems that travel horizontally outwards from the main plant before sending new shoots upwards.

Flower

Bud

Divided leaf

Stolon
(rooted
underground
stem)

Roots

**CHRYSANTHEMUM
PLANT**

**CROSS-SECTION OF TYPICAL
SINGLE CHRYSANTHEMUM
INFLORESCENCE**

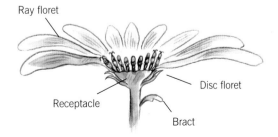

Ray floret

Disc floret

Receptacle

Bract

Chrysanthemum classification

In the UK, chrysanthemums have been divided by the National Chrysanthemum Society into three groups, based on unprotected garden growing and their flowering time. Of most relevance to the half-hardy floristry or exhibition forms, this classification refers to the point at which they start flowering and when they are likely to be curtailed by frost. There is then a range of subdivisions, based on habit, flower type and color.

Since hardy chrysanthemums can be treated like any other garden perennial, this is usually of secondary interest to the average gardener, who just wants a good plant to grow. It is, however, much more relevant in the cutting patch and is critical on the show bench.

When it comes to home-growing and understanding how the plant naturally operates, the picture is magnificently confused by the perpetual presence of cut chrysanthemum flowers and potted nursery stock, much of which will have been brought on out of season. But the key takeaways are that the cultivars that naturally flower early, before the frosts, can be grown in the garden, as can the hardy perennial varieties. Those that come into bloom later in the season and which are also frost-tender, will need protection if they are to put on a good show.

The explanation below is a generalization, applying mostly to exhibition forms, and with 30 different classifications and many thousands of cultivars, there is bound to be some variability. But understanding the terminology and how it is applied are key to both making use of the classification system and also to managing without if it is not relevant to you.

Classification is primarily designed to help the grower of show chrysanthemums decide which registered flowers they want to exhibit and what class or category is suitable. Where chrysanthemums have not been registered, as many hardy and commercial ones are not, no "official" categorization exists.

A general overview of how this works in the UK and US is given below and more information is available from the resources on p.42. It is worth noting that different countries may apply different systems of categorization.

In its simplest form, a cultivar is described as either early, mid-season or late flowering, then assessed according to shape, size and a range of other specific qualities.

Early These chrysanthemums naturally bloom from late summer and are considered to last until the early autumn. In practice, this is based on a guess at the date of the first frost, but with a changing climate meaning that frost may not arrive until chronological winter is well underway, they can go on and on. These may or may not need to be overwintered indoors or otherwise protected, depending on the hardiness of the cultivar in question and the nature of the site.

Mid-season Flowering from early autumn until late autumn, their defining quality is that they arrive between the early and the late cultivars. In practice, they have been traditionally used as a garden flower, rather like dahlias; planted in garden soil, they bloom until the frost, and they are then lifted and brought inside to overwinter, or if they are in pots, to carry on blooming.

Late These plants flower from late autumn to midwinter. Grown in pots, they can live outside until frost is imminent and then be brought inside to bloom. Alternatively, they can be grown in the greenhouse border.

With exhibition convention driving the order in which the categories are assigned, at first glance these appear idiosyncratic. While logic would dictate that the numbers should start low and climb as the season progresses, the late-flowering forms are, in fact, in the lowest-numbered classes. So, when viewed from the chronological perspective of a normal garden, the whole thing is upside down.

As discussed on p.26, flowering time is divided into Early, Mid-season or Late, where the plant starts flowering in early, mid- or late autumn. Large, medium or small flowers are then indicated by the letters a, b and c.

From this point, things get more complex. There are also a number of sub-sections indicating flower shape; these are:

a – Anemone
b – Pompon
c – Reflexed
d – Singles
e – Intermediate
f – Spiders, Quills and Spoons, and other

But a given flower shape can be in multiple groups: Pompons can be Early, Mid-season or Late, for example, and a group can cover e.g. Incurved and Reflexed flowers, as in section 1 (see below), or all of large, medium and small flowers, as in section 23. Spiders, Quills and Spoons are often collectively referred to as Fantasy types.

There are also further subcategories, where, for example, in subcategory f, Spiders are "a," Quills are "b" and Spoons are "c," while Pompons can be classed as rounded "full" Pompons, or "semi" Pompons, which are shaped like an upturned bowl, or half-sphere.

UK Chrysanthemum Sections as published by the National Chrysanthemum Society

LATE OR INDOOR FLOWERING

1. Large Exhibition
2. Medium Exhibition
3. Exhibition Incurved
4. Reflexed Decoratives
5. Intermediate Decoratives
6. Anemone
7. Singles
8. Pompons ("a" being true or full pompons and "b" being semi-pompons)
9. Spray varieties
10. Spiders, Quills and Spoons
11. Other types
12. a) Charms and b) Cascades

MID-SEASON; GARDEN OR GREENHOUSE FLOWERING

13. Incurved
14. Reflexed
15. Intermediate
16. Large October Flowering
17. Singles
18. Pompons
19. Spray varieties
20. Any other types
21. Hardy Garden Chrysanthemums

EARLY; OUTDOOR OR GARDEN FLOWERING

22. Early garden flowering charms
23. Incurved
24. Reflexed
25. Intermediate
26. Anemone
27. Single
28. Pompons
29. Spray varieties
30. Any other types

US Chrysanthemum Classes

Class 1 – Irregular Incurve
Class 2 – Reflex
Class 3 – Incurve
Class 4 – Decorative
Class 5 – Intermediate Incurve
Class 6 – Pompon
Class 7 – Single & Semi-Double
Class 8 – Anemone
Class 9 – Spoon
Class 10 – Quill
Class 11 – Spider
Class 12 – Brush & Thistle
Class 13 – Unclassified (Exotic)

As mentioned earlier, other than acting as an indication of hardiness, this categorization system is primarily of interest to exhibitors. Chrysanthemum societies and suppliers' websites (see p.42) give detailed information and further explanations of how the system works.

Notes on classification

In the UK, it is the large and medium forms that are colloquially described as "Japanese." In sections 3 to 7, and 13 to 15, a = large flowered, b = medium flowered, c = small flowered.

Rather like hardiness ratings, UK and US systems do not align exactly, with sizes in the US being assigned a letter from AA to C, large to small. To draw a further parallel between the American and British terminology, a Regular Incurve would be British sections 3, 13 or 23, depending upon whether the flower arrived in November, October or September, respectively. An Irregular Incurve would be British sections 5, 15 or 25.

COLOR IN CLASSIFICATION

When they are registered, chrysanthemums are assigned an official color which is often appended to their classification. Since photographs and descriptions amply address color in this book, the registered color has been omitted in the profiles Since photographs and descriptions amply address color in this book, the registered color has been omitted in the profiles.

The six main colors are Bronze, Pink, Purple, Red, Yellow and Salmon; each of these can be Light or Deep. Added to this are White, Cream and Other Colors in the UK. 'John Hughes' (p.80) would therefore be 13b W and 'John Riley' (p.129) would be 14b R.

Flower forms

Chrysanthemum flowers vary in shape and size and, as can be seen in pages 46–211, they change as they expand and mature; this is one of the qualities that makes them beguiling. Some varieties show an attractive tendency for the bloom to change color – sometimes quite dramatically – as it ages. This feature is particularly prevalent in the hardier cultivars.

The extensive array of flower forms ranges from adaptable decorative blooms to vast flowers perfect for exhibition, and these include all sorts of intriguing styles, such as the exotic Spider chrysanthemums and unusual Brush and Thistle varieties. Below is a selection of key flower forms, according to the classification system on pp.26–29.

Single

This is the simplest form of chrysanthemum flower and the one that most resembles other members of the daisy family. A single ring of petals, or ray florets, is arranged around a central boss of disc florets. They are usually grown as sprays of smaller blooms for garden or floristry use, although there is an exhibition class for them, too.

The term "single" is, in fact, rather loose. It is often applied to flowers with two, three or even five rows of petals, and can stray into the nebulous realms of semi-double, but the key thing is the open form and visible disc in the middle of the flower. Among aficionados of hardy garden chrysanthemums, flowers with two rows of petals, such as the one pictured, are sometimes referred to as "duplex."

Incurved

These flowers form perfect globes of petals because the florets arc upwards and overlap smoothly and evenly in the mature bloom. Incurved blooms can be small and medium-sized, and they can also be represented by the impressive Large Exhibition types, which are spectacular but tricky to grow.

Incurved flowers for showing in the UK tend to be tighter in form than those in the US, which means that you don't see the color on the inside of the petal.

INCURVED

SINGLE

Reflexed

Chrysanthemum flowers that are Reflexed have petals that open up and bend backwards to create a full but fairly flat top to the flower, and a long, dense waterfall of petals around the rim of the bloom. When fully Reflexed, the flower makes a neat ball, just like the Incurved varieties but in reverse. When picked prior to full maturity, the indeterminate direction of the petals gives the flowers a decadent swirling quality which lends them well to floristry.

INTERMEDIATE

REFLEXED

Intermediate

These fully double, loosely spherical flowers have shorter florets which also curve less strongly, producing a fairly open flower which may close at the top. This form is common in chrysanthemums produced for commercial floristry.

Decorative

Particularly pretty and abundantly well suited to cutting, Decorative chrysanthemums have shorter petals than fully Incurved or Reflexed forms; their base is rounded but because the central florets curve inwards and the outer ones are usually reflexed, they appear somewhat flattened on top. Fully double with no central disc, they have a lush, inviting appearance, which makes them desirable and extremely adaptable blooms. In the US this is a category in its own right, while in the UK this shape sits in sections 4, 14 and 24 and also 5, 15 and 25, which are Reflexed and Intermediate chrysanthemums.

DECORATIVE

Anemone

With one or several rings of petals around a prominent dome of disc florets, Anemone chrysanthemums look very much like an old-fashioned powder puff. The center of the flower may be tightly packed like the Single forms or, where the disc florets have part-formed petals, it may be looser and fluffier. This quality can sometime create an attractive contrast, as in Yellow Bokaa (see p.208).

ANEMONE

Pompon

Adaptable filler flowers in a posy, Pompons are widespread in both commercial production and as hardy garden plants. They may be fully globular or hemispherical, with a flat bottom, as in the Semi-Pompon, pictured. In chrysanthemums, this type of bloom tends to be fairly small at under 4 inches, even when disbudded, and they are often very much smaller. Obscuring the center of the flower, the tightly packed petals are part-furled and arranged in an expanding spiral that opens and reflexes as the flower matures, to create the classic drumstick shape.

POMPON

Spoon

A Single or Semi-Double chrysanthemum with attitude, these flowers are made up of several layers of tubular quills pointing out from the round central hub like spokes on a bicycle wheel. Each quill opens out to a flat, spatulate or curved tip – hence the name – and because chrysanthemum petals are often a brighter color on their upper side than they are on the back, this creates a striking effect.

Spider

One of the most dramatic and iconic chrysanthemum forms, Spiders have long, tubular florets, often with a hook at the end. The bore of the tube varies from very narrow and slender to much heavier and coarser, and as the flower matures, these splay or coil depending on variety. These often earn their Fantasy status magnificently.

Quill

Like Spoons and Spiders, Quill chrysanthemums are categorized as Fantasy blooms. Fully double and blessed with punky, explosive qualities, this type of chrysanthemum is highly desirable for its good looks and floral energy. The name is appropriately descriptive; the flower has petals that are long and straight with a slanted open end, and when flower arranging is the order of the day, Quills can be used anywhere a Cactus dahlia would also be at home.

SPOON

QUILL

SPIDER

Developing new cultivars

While named cultivars are conserved through vegetative propagation, growing plants from seed offers the possibility of creating something new and exciting and, in chrysanthemums, variable chromosome numbers and polyploidy permit a high level of flexibility. When cross-pollination occurs, the resulting seedlings will differ from the parent plants, and while some may be unremarkable, a few may be improvements.

Directed breeding is achieved by hybridizing known varieties and related plants. This is the means by which the original ornamental cultivars were created in ancient China and Japan, with further work done in the west after their introduction. Later, crosses between the existing complex hybrids and *Chrysanthemum zawadazkii* produced the hardy forms.

In this process, pollen is transferred from the anthers of one plant to the stigma of another with a small, soft paintbrush, and the seed parent is then isolated so no further pollination can occur. In the first years of the twenty-first century, this

led to some of the exciting modern commercial flowers, through crossing existing floristry blooms with other *Chrysanthemum* species and related plants. The resulting hybrids were then improved, and the "new" types included amazing green forms such as 'Anastasia Green', which has related *Ajania pacifica*, sometimes known as *Chrysanthemum pacifica*, in its DNA.

Alternatively, new chrysanthemums can arise from natural "sports," where a mutation causes a noticeable change in part or all of the plant. This often results in alterations to flower color or shape, and taking a cutting from the mutated section and growing it on may lead to innovative cultivars. Pink flowers are particularly useful as all other colors can then arise from these as sports.

Commercial chrysanthemum breeders use this quality to their advantage, often irradiating cuttings to actively create mutations, then monitoring the plants for interesting developments. Because the radiation mutates the flower color, often without changing the other characteristics of the clone, the resulting product is consistent. A large producer such as Dekker Chrysanten in the Netherlands will assess hundreds of thousands of seedlings annually, before selecting a fairly small number to release commercially.

Chrysanthemums as cut flowers

Chrysanthemums are one of the best-known cut flowers in the world. Even when they are perceived as unfashionable, there is no doubt that they excel in arrangements and they can often last at least two weeks in water.

Ideally, harvest flowers first thing in the morning, when the air is cool and the cells of the plant are plump and turgid. Choose blooms which are expanding and showing some color, or in the case of spray chrysanthemums, when around one in four flowers is open. Cut the stems long, plunging them straight into a bucket of clean, cold water, and when you have finished, trim the stalks again, under water. Then put the bucket of flowers somewhere cool and shady so they can have a drink and recover, leaving them for several hours or overnight.

The technique is then the same for both shop-bought and home-grown blooms. Strip off surplus lower leaves which can compete with the flower for water, and cut the stems at a 45-degree angle, ideally under water to stop air bubbles forming. Then arrange in a vase with a few drops of white vinegar or bleach to slow bacterial growth and make the flowers last longer. Change the water and add a fresh dash of vinegar every three to four days, or as necessary, trimming the stems each time and discarding any that are looking tired.

Whether in single-variety bunches or combined with other seasonal flowers and foliage, chrysanthemums have impact. They also work well displayed as a series of stems in individual bottles, where they will benefit from a lack of crowding and plenty of ventilation. As with all cut flowers, they will last best if kept in a cool place, out of direct sunlight and away from drafts and hot radiators.

Designing with chrysanthemums

For all their abundance in floristry, the revival of chrysanthemums as a garden plant is long overdue. Amongst perennials, almost nothing else will start flowering at the end of summer and potentially keep going until the earliest spring bulbs poke up their noses. And very little else will provide the range and intensity of color, either.

To get the most out of chrysanthemums outdoors, make sure that the plants get what they need in terms of sunshine and drainage, then use them as you wish. The more compact varieties and those plants which form mounds and cushions are known for making good pot plants, so use them in containers either by themselves or combined with other flowers, such as geraniums or lobelia, or with foliage such as heuchera, tiarella or ivy. They also look well with grasses, or even small shrubs.

In areas with higher rainfall or on heavy soil, consider chrysanthemums in raised beds. These provide good drainage and allow the moisture-sensitive cultivars to flower for longer, despite winter wet, while the plants can be encouraged to sprawl and cascade over the side in a gay waterfall of bloom. Unless the location is fairly sheltered, however, it is wise to choose reliably cold-tolerant varieties, since a raised bed is essentially just a large container and the elevated position can increase exposure to frost.

In the open border, chrysanthemums look fantastic when woven through other seasonal plants, taking their place alongside salvias, cannas, dahlias and ginger lilies or basking in front of a warm wall covered in roses and rosehips. Bold, bright varieties can be used to provide a vibrant counterpoint to grasses, and they can be interspersed with annual sunflowers and tagetes to create a flaming autumn display. The more subtle, creamy hues can also be teamed with the white trumpets of nicotiana and other light-colored flowers.

For something a bit more unexpected, allow the tallest and leggiest chrysanthemum cultivars to scramble up an obelisk, tying in as required, where they act as a surprisingly effective late-season alternative to a small-flowered clematis.

Societies and organizations

The historical popularity of chrysanthemums has left a legacy of organizations that remain dedicated to this most fabulous of blooms. National societies and chrysanthemum collections exist on almost every continent, and specialist suppliers also shoulder the burden of making sure that new enthusiasts are well supplied and well informed.

Commercial blooms, too, are produced in many countries of the world, notably in Africa and Asia, as well as in Colombia, the Netherlands and a range of other locations, and this creates hubs of specific expertise.

To find out more about chrysanthemums, a local club is a great place to start, and look out for regional exhibitions and events. Growers and nurseries may also have open days.

UK
National Chrysanthemum Society
https://chrysanthemum-ncs.org

Hardy Plant Society
www.hardy-plant.org.uk

Plant Heritage
www.plantheritage.org.uk

Norwell Nurseries
www.norwellnurseries.co.uk

Halls of Heddon
www.hallsofheddon.com

Chrysanthemums Direct
www.chrysanthemumsdirect.co.uk

The RHS Plantfinder is also useful when tracking down particular varieties, www.rhs.org.uk

USA
National Chrysanthemum Society, USA
https://mums.org/

KINGSMUMS LLC
www.kingsmums.com

Harmony Harvest Farm has a Mums Project dedicated to revitalizing interest in heritage chrysanthemums and their economic potential as a cut flower
www.hhfshop.com

Australia and New Zealand
New Zealand National Chrysanthemum Society Inc.
www.chrysanthemumsnz.weebly.com

The Western Australian Chrysanthemum Society Inc.
www.chrysanthemumwa.com

France, Germany, Netherlands
Conservatoire National du Chrysanthème Paul Lemaire in Ville de Saint-Jean de Braye near Orléans, France
www.ccvs-france.org

Lahr Chrysanthemum Festival, Germany
www.chrysanthema.de

Perennial Plant Nursery De Hessenhof, Netherlands
https://www.hessenhof.nl/index_en.htm

Notes on the plant profiles, pages 46–211

The aim of this book, like the rest of the Beautiful Varieties series, is to address the genus *Chrysanthemum* as broadly as possible, in a manner that is useful to gardeners, florists and anyone who enjoys lovely things. As a result, some technical or specific information has been standardized for the purpose, or omitted for ease of use. Should more details be required on any flower type or group, readers can refer to the resources opposite.

Flower size

When it comes to size of bloom, chrysanthemums are classified as Small, Medium or Large in the UK, while in the US they are assigned a letter from AA (very large) to C (small), but the precise size varies between categories. For home-growers and florists, the profiles on the following pages refer to the sizing below. This should be taken as a very rough indication as when plants are disbudded and secondary flowers removed, the remaining flower will be larger than if the flowers were grown as a spray.

Small: 1¼–2 in
Medium: 2½–4 in
Large: 4–8 in
Very large: over 8 in

Where relevant, plant heights have been indicated in the text.

Flowering period

Flowers are typically categorized as Early, Mid-season or Late (see p.26), unless they are produced All Year Round. Here we have broadly related flowering time to its season, to standardize between the hardy garden perennial chrysanthemums and the half-hardy florists' and exhibition categories, and to make sense of the seasons in both hemispheres. Approximate timings are indicated as below.

	Northern hemisphere	Southern hemisphere
Late summer	July–August	January– February
Early autumn	September–October	March–April
Mid-autumn	October	April
Late autumn	October–November	April–May
Early winter	November– December	May–June
Midwinter	January	July

Chic

May Shoesmith

If ever there was a chrysanthemum designed to turn heads and cause even the most phobic and cynical observer of the genus to question their convictions, that chrysanthemum is Shoesmith.

Almost decadent in their perfection, the large flowers make a dramatic focal feature with dense, curled petals that surround a greenish central dimple. Yet they are possibly even better massed together in a vase, their edges catching the light like the tops of thunder clouds on the horizon, while simultaneously looking every bit as soft, cuddly and tactile as a basket of snowy poodle puppies.

The name refers to Harry Shoesmith of Woking, Hampshire, UK. A horticulturist of note, he bred many outstanding show chrysanthemums over a long and distinguished career and was awarded the Victoria Medal of Honour by the Royal Horticultural Society.

A number of members of the Shoesmith family are immortalized in chrysanthemum form, including Elizabeth Shoesmith, which is an exotic, two-tone bloom the color of blackberries and cream, and Fred Shoesmith, which is a clear white Intermediate. There is also Yellow Fred Shoesmith, which is a sport of the original plant and therefore, according to the regulations of the British National Chrysanthemum Society, its name must contain at least part of the name of the parent cultivar.

Over the years, many sports have arisen from the original plants, and it is likely that they have been used in commercial development too. It can now be hard to track down which descendent of which Shoesmith is delighting the eye, but the fine qualities that originally defined flowers from the august stable of Harry Shoesmith live on.

Flower type Exhibition and floristry
Flowering period Late autumn and early winter
Hardiness rating USDA Zone 9; RHS H2
Form Intermediate
Flower size Large
Color Clear white with a touch of green
How to use Shoesmith is best brought on under glass where it will produce late flowers for cutting or for show
Alternative varieties White Fairweather and the creamier, looser-flowered White Cassandra will flower around the same time; for flowers around two months earlier, try White Billy Bell, which is classified as 15a in the UK and 5A in the US.

Gustav

Autumn is often associated with a palette of bronze, terracotta and gold, but purple is a color with infinite potential, and Gustav confounds seasonal expectations by bouncing into the room with a vivid color, visual vigor, and a bloom that stands out magnificently among the rank and file.

In chrysanthemums, a pompon shape is not unusual, but the flowers are often small and they are generally associated with sprays of dainty buttons or dense cushions of bloom. Gustav, however, is a modern commercial introduction which produces large, bold globes that can be up to 2¾ inches across, in an arrestingly sassy hue.

With a bit of imagination and considerable sartorial flair, Gustav could be deployed as a statement buttonhole. Alternatively, capitalize on the sweet vibrancy of the flower to lift more subtle companions. Use it to add a jolt to the antique magenta and teal of aging hydrangea blooms or team with the spare mahogany stems of dried sedum (*Hylotelephium*) and dangling Chinese lanterns *(Physalis alkekengi),* softened with lots of evergreen foliage and tawny turning leaves.

....

Flower type Commercially grown florists' variety
Flowering period Available all year round as a cut flower
Hardiness rating USDA Zone 9; RHS H3
Form Pompon
Flower size Medium
Color Purple
How to use Throw into a contrasting glazed jug for a welcome splash of color to brighten a room on a dull winter's day
Alternative varieties Andrea and Barca Purple are commercially available blooms which also show a good, strong purple color; in the garden, Rosetta (see p.166) produces pretty pink pompons over a long period

Fleur de Lis

One of the core varieties driving the new upswelling of interest in all things *Chrysanthemum*, Fleur de Lis is gorgeous, spectacular and deservedly popular.

The sort of thing that floral dreams are made of, this Fantasy bloom has slender quills that expand gradually like a slow-motion firework, cascading outwards and downwards to become nothing short of magnificent. The fine, glossy florets are magenta in youth, and lighten to a cheerful, zingy purple as they lengthen and mature, each one tipped with a neat hook for an effect that is both delicate and impactful.

The name is a slight conundrum as the fleur-de-lis is generally used as a heraldic symbol or design motif and in that instance, it refers to a lily flower, which at first glance seems a long way from the spreading and classically spidery qualities of this chrysanthemum. Yet the packed center of the flower does tend to stand quite erect and the quills do arch downwards, so in the eye of the beholder there may be some resemblance. Whatever the case, it is very fine indeed.

Fleur de Lis is classified as 11a in the US and 10a in the UK.

....

Flower type Exhibition and floristry
Flowering period Mid-autumn
Hardiness rating USDA Zone 9; RHS H3
Form Spider
Flower size Large to very large
Color Vibrant purple
How to use Disbud the stems to the terminal bud to create show-stopping focal blooms for arrangements; also suitable for exhibition
Alternative varieties For flowers destined for weddings, celebrations and other events, Kyoji, Seatons Galaxy, Vienna Waltz and Salhouse Dream perform a similar role

River City

Named after Sacramento in California, River City was bred and introduced by Leland Theodore King, whose eponymous nursery was situated nearby. Now legendary among stateside chrysanthemum lovers, the original King's Mums nursery ran from 1954 to 2008, and over this period, Ted took his hobby of collecting the best and most fascinating chrysanthemums he could lay his hands on and turned it into a thriving business. But he didn't just supply plants; he also bred and selected new varieties, too.

River City is one of his best-known introductions. A creature of beauty, its neat bronze buds open into a relaxed cascade of silky petals of an intriguing and enchanting hue. Descriptions vary – some enthusiasts say that the flowers evoke a sybaritic banquet of smoked salmon and champagne, while others suggest a cocktail of peach, orange, apricot and wine – and though the precise color may vary according to temperature and the age of the flower, this chrysanthemum is supremely popular.

Like all chrysanthemums, River City lends itself well to cutting and the plants remain compact, so it can also be grown in containers. It is classified as 1a, "Irregular Incurve" in the US.

....

Flower type Exhibition and floristry
Flowering period Mid- to late autumn
Hardiness rating USDA Zone 9; RHS H3
Form Incurved
Flower size Large
Color A lovely combination of peach, rose and salmon
How to use A really exemplary cut flower, its mutable, variable hues will go with almost everything; the largest blooms are achieved by disbudding, but growing as a spray creates flowers of an arguably more usable size
Alternative varieties William Florentine; Salmon Allouise blooms about a month earlier

Sweetheart Pink

If what you want is a chrysanthemum that thinks it's a dahlia, with strong stems and perfectly formed flowers, and with a bloom large enough to have impact but sufficiently lightweight for a blushing bride to carry with her all day, then look no further than Sweetheart Pink.

The flowers are fairly substantial for a hardy chrysanthemum and if florist–growers can get hold of it, the long blooming time makes it a must-have. It is, however, extremely difficult to find.

Peachy pink buds open to reveal shell-pink flowers just touched with sandy ochre, and the soft, rosy palette of faded coral and butterscotch cream bleaches elegantly as the bloom ages.

Sweetheart Pink was introduced by the famous British chrysanthemum nursery Johnsons of Tibshelf in 1940. Classified as 24b P, it was given an Award of Merit by the NCS at that time.

Flower type Hardy garden plant
Flowering period Early to late autumn
Hardiness rating USDA Zones 8–9; RHS H4
Form Double
Flower size Medium
Color Blush pink
How to use Use as you would a dahlia, rose or peony in a hand-tied bouquet, or arrange single stems in slender, intentionally mismatched glass vases
Alternative varieties Beechcroft (see p.154) has similar qualities in a single flower as do the Garden and Exhibition Spray chrysanthemums Honey Enbee Wedding, Percy Salter and Peach Southway Sheba

Mocha

Lovely Mocha is the sort of flower that goes with everything, but which is so unusual and variable in hue that nobody is quite sure what color it actually is.

There are indeed elements of cream and coffee, and of steaming froth dusted with chocolate, yet there are also notes of burnt raspberry-bronze, and in some cases, there is a slightly metallic or rusty tint as well. Where the florets curl up at the tips, meanwhile, their open mouths are revealed to be daubed with pink-mahogany.

When fully expanded, Mocha is a classically rounded Spider form, and as such, it does make a beautiful exhibition bloom. For floristry work, however, it is often better to nip out the top bud and encourage the plant to grow sprays of smaller blooms. These can be picked before they are fully mature, at a point when the loosely random and informal quills can give the arrangement energy and interest without being too full-on.

Mocha is a half-hardy perennial, classified as 11a in the US and 10a in the UK. Although it blooms prolifically, the stems are not as robust as those of some other chrysanthemums and it benefits from the protection of a greenhouse or polytunnel. If grown in the garden, the plant will need to be brought under cover in late autumn as a protection from frost.

....

Flower type Exhibition and floristry
Flowering period Late autumn
Hardiness rating USDA Zone 9; RHS H3
Form Spider
Flower size Large to very large
Color Dusty salmon, coffee and pink
How to use Grow as many as you can and cut by the armful for arranging; if your plant thrives, try your luck with exhibiting them, too
Alternative varieties Try Senkyo Kenshin (see p.180), and Judith Baker; varieties such as Tula Carmella and Baltazar Flame may not be quite as dramatic but can be bought as cut stems from the florist shop

Topspin

Naming plants often provides plant breeders with an opportunity to showcase their enthusiasm for their subject, and the whimsically titled Topspin, which refers to expert ball control in sport, brings with it more athletic analogies and anthropomorphisms than you can shake a stick at.

In the back room of the marketing department at Dekker Chrysanten in the Netherlands, the copywriters have had a field day, as it were, describing their bodacious bloom as being akin to a rising sports star, a champion with a promising future and a plant which plays a blinder without breaking a sweat.

Fortunately, the flower lives up to the hype. Its brilliant white quills radiate from a pale pistachio center, and the blooms contrast well with the deep green foliage below. And, as a useful cut flower, it performs as advertised, in a bold, handsome, no-fuss sort of way. Whether used in a vase, wreath or bridal bouquet, Topspin works hard and plays hard, and without a doubt it is one of life's winners.

Flower type Commercially grown florists' variety
Flowering period Available all year round as a cut flower
Hardiness rating USDA Zone 9; RHS H3
Form Double
Flower size Medium
Color Glistening white
How to use Available commercially as a spray or as a disbud; Topspin has excellent vase-life
Alternative varieties As cut stems, Celestial White, Chrystal White and Santini Spider are also good; for a garden variety, consider White Gem

Lili Gallon

Possibly a fairly old variety, Lili Gallon appears to have originated in France and made its way around the world. At some point, it arrived in the US and it has also been registered in the UK, but this must presumably have been prior to the globalization of cut-flower production, which saw robust, easy-to-transport varieties prioritized, while the international exchange of plants was restricted more generally.

In the UK, Lili Gallon is registered as a "Section 2 Medium Exhibition Purple," while in the US it falls into class 13, "Exotic and Unclassified," or chrysanthemums that do not fall into any other group. And, with its long, curled florets that are a deep ruby on one side and a cloudy pink on the other, it is certainly a striking plant, if not as tall as some.

Despite being nominally widespread, Lili Gallon is now a distinctly unusual bloom, and this specimen was, in fact, photographed in her home country at the Conservatoire National du Chrysanthème Paul Lemaire in Saint-Jean-de-Braye near Orleans, France. But thanks to the energy and interest of a small number of growers, particularly in the US, this chrysanthemum remains available and she definitely has her fans.

When plants migrate, they frequently find themselves with a new name – or a variation to their old name. This is often due to a simple error from, perhaps, the poor handwriting of the sender who wrote the label, or a mis-hearing of something unfamiliar. As a result, Lili Gallon is often listed as either Lili Callon or Lily Gallon, but despite this, she remains unmistakable.

....

Flower type Exhibition and floristry, heritage variety
Flowering period Late autumn
Hardiness rating USDA Zone 9; RHS H3
Form Reflexed
Flower size Very large
Color Wine-red and silver-pink
How to use A fascinating oddity rather than a floristry staple, perhaps, Lili Gallon will make a good focal bloom, and used as a single-variety arrangement, it will be a talking point
Alternative varieties When picked young, Kokka Bunmi has a similar freeform quality; as a cut stem, Vienna Pink and Vienna Copper are popular for their long, curly petals; Heritage bloom Duc de Bordeaux has an attractive lavender-and-white color scheme, but it is vanishingly rare

Emperor of China

A chrysanthemum of almost legendary status, Emperor of China is a beautiful creature indeed.

The fully double flowers expand from rosy buds to form stars of quilled petals in a delicate silver-rose with a darker, crimson-purple center. As the year fades and the temperature drops, the aromatic foliage adds to the autumn display, becoming suffused with an attractive russet, or sometimes even beetroot-red color, which adds considerably to the charms of the plant both in the garden and when picked for a vase.

Emperor of China is sometimes described as a Rubellum chrysanthemum, but this category didn't really exist until the breeding work of British nurseryman Amos Perry in the late 1920s. And, since the variety was mentioned both by doyenne of garden design, Gertrude Jekyll, in her book of 1888, and by wild gardener, William Robinson, in his earlier publication, around 1880, Emperor of China pre-dates the arrival of these by some margin.

This neatly illustrates some of the complexities inherent in consistently describing chrysanthemums, and Emperor of China could actually be older still. Its alternative name is Cottage Pink, and as plantswoman Margery Fish wrote in her book *Cottage Garden Flowers*, "There are certain, rather ordinary, good-tempered chrysanthemums that have come to be known as 'Cottage Pink' or 'Cottage Bronze', because at one time they were found in every cottage garden."

The plant grows to around 36 inches; it benefits from staking and should be mulched in winter. Resistant to white rust, it also tolerates winter wet reasonably well.

....

Flower type Hardy garden chrysanthemum, 21 ft
Flowering period Mid- to late autumn
Hardiness rating USDA Zones 7–9; RHS H5
Form Double
Flower size Medium
Color Silver-pink
How to use A resilient garden plant and an outstanding cut flower
Alternative varieties Lady in Pink is a paler, more open flower on a plant that is a true Rubellum, produced by Amos Perry in 1952; Tickled Pink is a hardy duplex spoon which flowers in early autumn

Vulpus

While some chrysanthemums stand the test of time and become well known, others are very much more obscure. Sports and mutations are a frequent occurrence, so populations tend to expand and vary, and because some plants are left behind, older private collections very often provide a snapshot of a particular period, and a window onto the living history of a group of plants.

The Beautiful Varieties series of books, of which this is one, explores many corners of the floral world, and we found Vulpus on a visit to the Conservatoire National du Chrysanthème Paul Lemaire in Saint-Jean-de-Braye near Orleans in France. The legacy of horticulturist and author Paul Lemaire, who died in 1978, this collection has been cared for ever since and was designated a National Collection in 1996.

The collection is diverse, containing hardy cultivars and chrysanthemums grown for cutting, as well as little "pomponettes" grown for seasonal decoration, but the bulk of the varieties are large-flowered blooms, many of which have all but vanished from wider cultivation.

Vulpus is, therefore, not a plant that can easily be acquired. The meaning of the name, too, is unclear, but it may be linked to an unusual European last name derived from the Latin word for "fox," *vulpes*, or a related reference to the color of the bloom.

....

Flower type Exhibition and floristry, heritage variety
Flowering period Late autumn
Hardiness rating USDA Zone 9; RHS H3
Form Intermediate
Flower size Very large
Color Distinctively foxy
How to use There are other fine rust-and-copper chrysanthemums that lend themselves to garden growing and floristry, but if you find yourself in France in the autumn, the Conservatoire is well worth a visit
Alternative varieties Early-flowering Hanenburg can be grown as a garden plant or bought as a containerized plant; San Tropez blooms a little later

Peach John Wingfield

Gorgeous, beguiling and supremely adaptable, Peach John Wingfield is one of those chrysanthemums which evolves over time, to deliver a series of aesthetic updates and pleasant surprises.

In an extremely promising start, the flower opens as if it were a Decorative form (see p.33), with petals that are dusty rose on the inside and champagne-pink to the reverse. At this perky point, it is a delightful addition to any bouquet or posy, but it has not yet hit its peak.

The petals then continue to lengthen and grow, gradually kinking backwards and backwards again, to create a full-on cascade that looks a little bit like a sugared, pale coral, floral waterfall.

Peach John Wingfield is officially classified as 2B in the US and 14b in the UK, which means that it is a mid-season, Reflexed chrysanthemum of medium size. It is a sport of the white John Wingfield, which is considered to be a reference variety for this category, and other sports include zesty yellow Sunny John Wingfield, which was introduced in 2011. These chrysanthemums tend to make stocky plants, reaching around 48 inches tall.

When grown for exhibition, the plants are normally "stopped" by removing the growing tip in mid-spring or early summer. The precise date is chosen to moderate the date of flowering so that the blooms are in peak condition to coincide with the relevant show (see p.229 for more information). Side buds are also removed, to maximize the size of the focal flower.

....

Flower type Exhibition and floristry
Flowering period Mid-autumn
Hardiness rating USDA Zone 9; RHS H3
Form Reflexed
Flower size Medium to large
Color Peach melba
How to use Superb exhibition variety and also makes a good cut flower for general use
Alternative varieties Peach Courtier, classified 24a in the UK and 2A in the US, is similar but flowers earlier; Percy Salter produces sprays of smaller flowers and is a good garden plant for early to mid-autumn

Gertrude

Just when you think that you have got to know chrysanthemums, and start to believe that you are getting on top of the almost infinite variations in form and of behavior, along comes Gertrude.

With her loosely incurved blooms of baby pink, a hint of apricot to the inner petals and a touch of lavender to the outer ones, she exudes an undeniable charm and an aesthetic that should win hearts with ease. But what really sets fair Gertrude apart are her distinctively hairy flowers.

Unexpected and almost disconcertingly fuzzy, the back of each of her petals is covered with fine, pale, silvered spikes, and these give the impression that the flower has been caught in a hard frost and the thaw is yet to come. But while this may distinguish Gertrude from her contemporaries, the feature is by no means unique. The Heritage French variety Oiseau de Paradis or Bird of Paradise also has spiny curls, and it is a quality that is starting to creep into the floristry trade, too. And the deeper you dig, the greater the oddities that can be found.

In Asia, for example, a variety called Hairy Thorns combines the prettiest pink-and-white coloring with chunky, curved, twisted tubular florets arranged like monstrous spiked stag's horns. It is weird, it is bizarre; it is not unlovely but it is certainly an acquired taste – and it goes to show, with chrysanthemums there is always something new.

....

Flower type Exhibition and floristry
Flowering period Mid-autumn
Hardiness rating USDA Zone 9; RHS H3
Form Incurved
Flower size Medium
Color Lovely pale pink
How to use The flowers can be grown in the garden until the first frost; they can also be used in mixed arrangements or displayed in individual vases, where their weirdness can be appreciated to the full
Alternative varieties The florist's form Cruella is a bronzy, spidery flower with a similar spikiness

John Hughes

Some chrysanthemums are classics of their kind and as an exhibition bloom, John Hughes is one of the varieties against which others are compared, both for form and for its neat and orderly arrangement of petals.

Grown as a spray of flowers destined to be picked young, the effect is relaxed and the creamy hue blends well with other pastel shades. This makes it a promising candidate for an autumn wedding where the often easier-to-source red and gold flowers are not invited.

When mature, the flowers form snowy spheres that are perfect for the show bench. A half-hardy perennial, John Hughes is treated as an indoor-flowering mid-season chrysanthemum, and the globular blooms are produced on an upright plant that grows to around 48 inches.

A good buttercream-colored sport, Yellow John Hughes (AGM), is also available. Like the original, this is also classified as 13b in the UK and 3B in the US.

Flower type Exhibition and floristry
Flowering period Mid-autumn
Hardiness rating USDA Zone 9; RHS H3
Form Incurved
Flower size Medium
Color Soft white
How to use As a show flower, restrict the blooms to just a couple on each plant and pay attention to stopping times in mid-spring or early summer (see p.229); the flowers can also be grown as a spray for cutting
Alternative varieties Yellow John Hughes is a sport of the original John Hughes; Kay Woolman and Lorna Wood are similar white chrysanthemums in the same class, while the earlier-flowering White Allouise can be grown in the garden for cutting

Seatons Ashleigh

Introduced by the legendary Australian chrysanthemum breeder Ron Seaton, this particularly fine Fantasy cultivar is named for his granddaughter, Ashleigh.

The color is magnificent – a glossy magenta-purple – and when the flower is fully open, the slender quills stick out in all directions just like a sea urchin. True to relaxed and practical antipodean form, Ron breeds all his chrysanthemums for both showing and cutting. Seatons Je'Dore (see p.86) is another excellent example of his work.

Although it is late-flowering, Seatons Ashleigh blooms over a relatively long period, and its narrow petals lend it a tolerance of wind and rain. It is classed as 10a in the US and 10b in the UK.

....

Flower type Exhibition and floristry
Flowering period Late autumn
Hardiness rating USDA Zone 9; RHS H3
Form Quill
Flower size Large
Color Magenta-purple
How to use Combine with acid-green flowers, mixed foliage and a few sprays of orange berries for a high-impact bouquet, or tone down with evergreen foliage and pink-and-teal antiqued hydrangea blooms
Alternative varieties Lola is a large, early-flowering lavender-pink quill, Tula Purple can be bought as a garden plant or as a potted specimen, while Pittsburgh™ Purple is a quilled pot mum

Graceful

Seatons Je'Dore

A classically gorgeous chrysanthemum with captivating blush blooms, Seatons Je'Dore is a good candidate for showing and cutting. And, since the very similar-sounding *J'adore* means "I love you" in French, its popularity with wedding florists comes as no surprise.

From the stable of renowned Australian breeders Ron and Lynn Seaton, the plants grow to around 40 inches high and 20 inches wide. They can be planted outdoors or under cover, depending on climate, but they do benefit from staking. The flowers start a gentle greenish apricot and mature to light pink, becoming paler and shaggier as they age.

Cut by the armful, these delectable champagne-bubble blooms are harmonious with a wedding dress of any hue. They combine beautifully with pastel spray roses, snapdragons and lisianthus, and they can be grown disbudded (see p.228) as fabulous focal flowers, or left *au naturel* for a daintier Spray.

Popular in its own land, Seatons Je'Dore is not reliably available internationally, but along with some of Ron and Lynn's other cultivars, it can be found in the US and India, which were export destinations before regulations on sending plants abroad were tightened. Elsewhere, a bit of focused research should throw up some decent local alternatives.

Flower type Exhibition and floristry
Flowering period Mid- to late autumn
Hardiness rating USDA Zone 9; RHS H3
Form Decorative
Flower size Medium to large
Color Pink-apricot
How to use Grow for cutting or for show
Alternative varieties Allouise Pink is similar but flowers a little earlier and the Kalimba Series (see p.144) can be bought as cut stems; experiment with Spray chrysanthemums such Peach Southway Sheba or Percy Salter

Saga No Yuki

Variety is a wonderful thing, and when the palate is jaded by the worthy but well-worn commercial cut flowers, and the mighty Exhibition blooms are just too ostentatious, the small, fine Brush and Thistle chrysanthemums provide something of an antidote.

These are the plants of connoisseurs, and when it comes to their naming conventions, they follow a logical path. Brush chrysanthemums are upright and punky, and look just like a charmingly raggedy paintbrush. Thistle chrysanthemums resemble a thistle flower – or even a part-formed seedhead. With a central fluff of florets surrounded by a querulous ring of rays, they look like the ghost of a famished Spider chrysanthemum – faint yet elegantly spare.

It is thought that flowers akin to simple and exquisite Saga No Yuki arose during and after the Heian period (794–1185) in Japanese history, which saw a great flourishing of art and culture. At this point, many new and exotic forms of chrysanthemum, or *kiku*, were cultivated, cementing both the iconic status of the flower and the distinctively dramatic Japanese style.

Saga No Yuki is classified as 12c in the US.

....

Flower type Exhibition and floristry
Flowering period Early to mid-autumn
Hardiness rating USDA Zone 9; RHS H3
Form Brush
Flower size Small
Color Silvery white
How to use If many flowers are available, they can be combined into a posy; however, a single, exquisite spray in a small vase is often the best way to appreciate the blooms
Alternative varieties There are a number of pretty Brush-type flowers, including Saga Nishiki, Saga No Izumi and Wisp of Pink

Salmon Fairweather

An utterly splendiferous, multi-purpose flower, Salmon Fairweather arrives late in the season, but it is certainly worth the wait.

To the one side, the petals are a delectable, nuanced, old-rose color, layered up and curling inwards like so many seashells. To the reverse, they are a sort of peachy, biscuit color with a hint of champagne and cream liqueur.

Stocky in stature and growing to around 40 inches (a meter) in height, Salmon Fairweather is a sport of the original Fairweather, which is a clear pink color, but has spawned a rainbow of mutant offspring, with White, Peach, Cream, Oyster and Bronze variants. Like all their class, these are indoor-flowering half-hardy perennials, but the blooms last for ages in a vase. Grown in large containers and brought inside as the weather deteriorates, they can flower right up until the festive season in some cases.

Salmon Fairweather is classified as 5b in the UK and 3(5)B in the US.

....

Flower type Exhibition and floristry
Flowering period Late autumn to early winter
Hardiness rating USDA Zone 9; RHS H3
Form Incurved
Flower size Large
Color Peachy pink
How to use A beautiful cut bloom, chrysanthemums in the Fairweather Group are also excellent for exhibition purposes
Alternative varieties Peach Fairweather is slightly darker in color; Salmon Allouise has earlier and more weatherproof incurved flowers, and these can be grown in the garden as well as under cover

PIP Pink

Where dahlias have blazed a trail of glamour and revelled in born-again popularity, chrysanthemums now go also. And when it comes to the PIP Series, it is easy to see why.

The flowers are a characteristic and adaptable Decorative shape, and the colors are exquisitely on trend, with deep, rich centers expanding into lighter-toned petals. These are then splashed and streaked with the deeper berry, coffee or caramel hues that underpin the overall scheme.

Modern commercial blooms developed with market success in mind, these particular chrysanthemums may not be in any way old-fashioned, but this is not necessarily a bad thing as they encapsulate every good quality imaginable. Combining utilitarian robustness, long vase-life and a pleasing form, the benefit of thorough breeding (see pp. 36–37) is that one can end up choosing from a palette of colors a little bit like a paint chart, and with red, orange and purple versions available, there is something to suit every room and lifestyle.

Flower type Commercially grown florists' variety
Flowering period Available all year round as a cut flower
Hardiness rating USDA Zone 9; RHS H3
Form Decorative
Flower size Medium
Color Shell-pink with blackcurrant splashes
How to use A good multi-purpose cut flower
Alternative varieties Commercial variety Serenity has a similar effect as does the VIP Series; hardy to half-hardy Spray chrysanthemums, such as the Pennine Group, which includes Pennine Point, Pennine Jane and Pennine Flute, can be grown as cutting-garden perennials

Fort Vancouver

Classifying flowers is a discipline that can border on an obsession for some horticulturists, and where a group of plants has been in cultivation for a long time, the systems used can become extensive and rather arcane. While this can lead to renewed rigor and some considerable debate, there are always plants that will fall outside the system. And, as a result, there is usually a catch-all group for "…and everything else."

Being hard to classify doesn't make a flower any less lovely, however, and although Fort Vancouver sits in the group that is labelled 13a, "Exotic or Unclassified" by the National Chrysanthemum Society, USA, it is still a joy to behold.

The flowers are large and somewhat lax, with substantial quills that are rich and heavy, wide open and scooped to the tips. And as the blooms mature and the florets relax backwards under the force of gravity, they open further still.

In youth, the bloom is a positively regal combination of dark pink-bronze with hints of deep violet, which tone well with other chrysanthemums, perhaps in hues of burnt orange and fizzy magenta, for a stylish autumn display.

Flower type Exhibition and floristry
Flowering period Late autumn
Hardiness rating USDA Zone 9; RHS H3
Form Quill
Flower size Large
Color Plum-bronze
How to use Magnificent Fort Vancouver works well when stems are disbudded to create a single, handsome focal flower for cutting
Alternative varieties River City has a similar relaxed charm, gentle coloring and similar requirements for growth, or try Judith Baker for a rich bronze glow

Jeanny Rosy

The little button blooms of Jeanny Rosy are typical of modern spray chrysanthemums; they are charming, long-lasting, and go with almost everything, and as a result, they have become a florist's favorite. With its shell-pink rim and greenish center, this particular flower is fairly muted and it is ideal for mixing with larger chrysanthemums in shades of pink, white or cream, combining with soft mauve asters and even as a foil for lilies.

Technically, the flower is titled Santini Jeanny Rosy and it is part of the Santini Series bred by Dekker Chrysanten. This is made up of a fairly wide range of florists' chrysanthemums which are characterized by cultivars that produce many small blooms in a dense spray. These lend themselves to posies and smaller arrangements that benefit from compact yet vibrant clusters of flowers. The name Jeanny, meanwhile, is a prefix of a specific range of Spray Pompon chrysanthemums which includes Jeanny Orange, Jeanny Purple, Jeanny Peach and Jeanny Cherry.

Flower type Commercially grown florists' variety
Flowering period All year round
Hardiness rating USDA Zone 9; RHS H3
Form Pompon
Flower size Small
Color Pink and pale green
How to use Jeanny Rosy goes with almost anything, so use as a filler flower in an eclectic bouquet
Alternative varieties Peter Magnus (see p.140) is a small Anemone-form flower, also in delicate pink, and which can be grown at home; Mavis (AGM) is a fairly hardy pink pompon for garden growing in a sheltered position

Syllabub

While some chrysanthemums wow with their magnificent size or intimidate with coiling cascades of tentacles, Syllabub is a vision of sweetness and perfection on a far more relatable scale. This is a chrysanthemum where the flowers are cute rather than concerning, but diminutive size notwithstanding, it is rich with detail and fine form.

Like honey-scented pink pinwheels, the blooms are captivating. Whorls of silver-gray quills tipped with hot pink spoons surround an Anemone center, and the flowers are carried on a plant where the impact of the many outweighs the small size of the individual.

Forming a spreading mound 24–28 inches wide and 24 inches tall, Syllabub is usually considered along with other hardy chrysanthemums, but in truth it is less hardy than some, and it is wise to give it a bit of winter protection, moving it into a cold greenhouse or covering with a fleece or blanket should temperatures plummet.

Classified as 21f in the UK, Syllabub sits in the Korean Group, due to its particular heritage (see p.20), and it received an RHS Award of Garden Merit in 2003.

....

Flower type Borderline hardy garden plant
Flowering period Early autumn
Hardiness rating USDA Zone 9; RHS H3
Form Quilled Spoon
Flower size Small
Color Pink and silver
How to use Grow in a container or raised bed; cuts well for posies and mixed arrangements
Alternative varieties Mavis Smith is a much tougher hardy plant, Tickled Pink is a paler pink duplex Spoon, while long-flowering Wendy Tench has dark pink flowers and more open, partly quilled petals

Capriool

Sweet in both color and demeanor, Capriool is a chrysanthemum for all seasons. The young flowers are greenish yellow at the center, but as the tightly furled petals expand, the clusters of airy tentacles become uniformly baby-pink, and fill the space with cheerful and light-hearted vibes.

Resembling a Cactus dahlia in both form and function, Capriool can be used in much the same way in floristry, where it will last for several weeks. Team with smaller pink- and white-toned flowers such as asters, gypsophila and cosmos, and add lashings of ferny or glaucous blue foliage.

The name Capriool is the Dutch form of the word "capriole," which refers to a little jump or playful caper, and is used in dance.

Flower type Commercially grown florists' variety
Flowering period Available all year round as a cut flower
Hardiness rating USDA Zone 9; RHS H3
Form Spider
Flower size Large
Color Bubble-gum pink
How to use Buy a bunch or three, and get creative
Alternative varieties Anastasia Pink, Cipria and Tula Sharletta are all useful flowers, which do more or less the same thing

Innocence syn. L'innocence

Raised in France as L'innocence, these charming, impactful flowers hold their own alongside all other kinds of daisy, and they are often considered to be pretty much bomb-proof in the garden.

Performing best in the middle of a border, the plant is around 24 inches tall and wide, with attractive dark green foliage. The flowers are held well-erect, and at the bottom of a single whorl of misty pink petals is a central boss of greenish gold. The plant benefits from being divided every few years in order to rejuvenate it.

Innocence was honored with an RHS Award of Garden Merit in 2012 and is classified in the UK as 21d.

....

Flower type Hardy garden plant
Flowering period Mid-autumn to early winter
Hardiness rating USDA Zones 7–9; RHS H5
Form Single
Flower size Medium
Color Blush-pink
How to use Plant in a sunny border to provide for bees, hoverflies and other pollinating insects
Alternative varieties Aunt Millicent is very similar and is often considered interchangeable, and Hebe is similar but more compact; Jolie Rose is a slightly deeper pink, while Alison and fuss-free Clara Curtis could also be considered; in the US, Coral Daisy is in the same sort of ball park

Bretforton Road

If what you want is a plant which is hardy and reliable, provides a great splash of color in a sunny spot, and cuts well for a supply of long-lasting flowers late in the season, then Bretforton Road is an excellent option.

The semi-double flowers have several lush layers of vivid, shocking pink petals surrounding a brilliant gold center, and they are carried over rich, aromatic, dark green foliage on a plant which does not get too tall. The distinctive shade of pink in the blooms looks particularly well with cerise, magenta and purple salvias, or with rosehips, grasses and the fading seedheads of summer blooms.

Classed as a Korean chrysanthemum, the plant was introduced by Bob Brown of Cotswold Garden Flowers in the UK, and named for the private garden in which it had been growing for many years.

....

Flower type Hardy garden plant
Flowering period Mid-autumn to early winter
Hardiness rating USDA Zones 7–9; RHS H5–6
Form Semi-double
Flower size Medium
Color Bright cerise
How to use Use to brighten the autumn border alongside Michaelmas daisies, sedums (*Hylotelephium*) and euphorbia
Alternative varieties The old variety Anastasia is a good, pink double chrysanthemum, Herbstkuss arrives rather earlier but does a similar job, while Mrs Jessie Cooper has fantastic hot pink flowers that keep going all the way into winter

Citronella

A name like Citronella generates certain expectations of a flower, and to its absolute credit, this is a chrysanthemum that lives up to the hype.

The small blooms are fully double and well-stuffed at that, and they carry with them the brisk, enticing scent of limoncello on ice. As one might anticipate, they are lemon-yellow in color but there is a touch of lime in the center when they are young. The scooped petals are paler to the reverse, meanwhile, which adds texture as the flower starts to mature and relax.

The plant has a well-branched and bushy habit and relatively compact proportions of 18–24 inches high and 24 inches wide. This means that it sits well fairly near the front of the border and lends itself to container gardening, too. It is weather-resistant, flowers throughout the autumn and copes with cold down to a very respectable 7°F, but it is worth paying attention to winter drainage on heavier soils.

Citronella was introduced by the nursery of famous German plantsman Karl Foerster, who is widely known because of the grass *Calamagrostis* 'Karl Foerster', which was named in his honor in 1977, seven years after his death.

....

Flower type Hardy garden plant
Flowering period Late summer to autumn
Hardiness rating USDA Zones 7–9; RHS H4–5
Form Double
Flower size Small to medium
Color Clear, zesty yellow
How to use Citronella makes an excellent cut flower
Alternative varieties Folksong has a honey-and-lemon scent, while Spartan Canary and Jante Wells have a good yellow color, if not the distinctive lemony fragrance

Purple Light

With super-funky flying saucers on top of sturdy stems, Purple Light is an eye-catching plant indeed.

The color of the blooms is fresh, clear and bright, and it will go with almost anything, and since they appear earlier than some exhibition-type chrysanthemums, there should be plenty of suitable companions to choose from. Look in the garden for phlox and stems of miscanthus, seek out late roses and *Echinacea*, and make the most of salvias and any remaining cosmos for cheerful, informal arrangements.

Although it is not winter-hardy, Purple Light can be grown outside as a middle-of-the-border plant in a sunny spot. It may well need staking in exposed areas or to prevent flopping. Lift in winter or otherwise protect from cold and wet.

Purple Light appeared as a sport of First Light – a chrysanthemum with a more gentle character, pinker and slightly grayer in color, that is evocative of early dawn. It is classified as 8a in the US.

Flower type Exhibition and floristry
Flowering period Early to mid-autumn
Hardiness rating USDA Zone 9; RHS H3
Form Anemone
Flower size Medium
Color Mauve-pink
How to use It will perform on the show bench if required, but it also looks great piled into a large jug with foraged loveliness from the garden
Alternative varieties Peter Magnus (see p.140) has a similar flower but smaller; other late Anemone forms include Mundial Rose and Jill Anderton

Vienna Copper

Fabulously fashionable and luxuriously louche, Vienna Copper has gained an ardent following in the few years since it was launched, and in many ways this is no surprise.

With gently warm autumnal hues, it has the same brown, pink and cream undertones as that most lauded of dahlias, Café au Lait. And its wide petals don't so much curve inwards as form loose and distinctive curls, each flower resembling a bunch of tousled ribbons – or a handful of linguini pasta, according to the less charitable.

Indeed, this is a bloom that looks not so much vintage as archaic, as if it had just stepped out of a painting or from some fragile and ancient printed silk. And with its heritage plain for all to see, it is much in demand at the more exclusive boutiques and in upper-class bouquets.

Along with its equally delectable siblings, Vienna Pink and Vienna White, Vienna Copper is only available at the time of writing as a cut flower; the stems usually disbudded to create a single, magnificent focal bloom.

Flower type Commercially grown florists' variety
Flowering period Late summer to late autumn
Hardiness rating USDA Zone 9; RHS H3
Form Intermediate
Flower size Large to very large
Color Faded copper-cream
How to use A really eye-catching cut flower, Vienna Copper makes an excellent focal point
Alternative varieties Peach Courtier and Apricot Alexis have a similar aesthetic and color but rather tidier bloom, while those lucky enough to be in Australia could look for Kath McKrabb

Timeless

John Riley

With pointed petals in rich, velvety, theatre-curtain red, the sumptuous flowers of
Chrysanthemum John Riley radiate like a burgundy sun around a dense-yet-expanding
solar core of younger petals that are brushed lightly with copper.

The petals incurve crisply on opening, but as the flower continues to grow, they lengthen
and relax, falling backwards in a domed and shaggy cluster evoking a drooping, tentacle-
heavy sea anemone at low tide.

A half-hardy perennial and thoroughly good all-rounder, John Riley is widely available
and has stood the test of time. Often cultivated under cover and disbudded to create a
single bloom for showing, it can also be left to grow naturally outdoors, which results in
plants that are just over 40 inches (a meter) tall with sprays of flowers that may be a little
smaller, but which are no less intensely lovely.

John Riley is classified as 14b in the UK.

Flower type Exhibition and floristry, sometimes commercially grown
Flowering period Early to mid-autumn
Hardiness rating USDA Zone 9; RHS H3
Form Reflexed
Flower size Large
Color Rich, deep red
How to use Fairly weather-resistant, John Riley can be grown to flower in the garden or
under cover; it cuts well and also lends itself to the show bench
Alternative varieties Harry Lawson, Doreen Statham and Domingo have a similar
flowering time, while Regal Mist Red is an earlier-flowering Incurved form

Fuego

When a massive shot of autumn drama is required, *Chrysanthemum* Fuego is hard to beat. The flowers are large and striking, with an eye-catching color scheme; the upper side of the petals is a deep caramel orange while the more conspicuous reverse is painted a glossy tangerine-gold, giving the impression of a flower that smolders and shimmers with heat.

The Spanish word for "fire," *fuego!* is sometimes used colloquially to indicate that something is figuratively on fire, in the sense of being brilliant, excellent or sexy. Unsurprisingly, the chrysanthemum delivers here, too in terms of its flaming loveliness, but as it is hard to do anything low-key with it, it is best not to try.

Fuego is a flower that cannot and should not be muted, so throw it into a vase and combine with every hot-colored plant you can lay your hands on – rosehips, early holly berries, autumn leaves and late, dark dahlias, then anchor the incendiary arrangement with the deepest shade of evergreen foliage available.

Flower type Commercially grown florists' variety
Flowering period Available for much of the year as a cut flower
Hardiness rating USDA Zone 9; RHS H3
Form Intermediate
Flower size Large
Color Copper and tangerine
How to use Buy a big bunch of cut stems and throw into a suitably unsubtle vase
Alternative varieties San Tropez is similar, while Australian variety Kellies Bonfire is an exciting variation on the theme; popular hardy chrysanthemum Etna has similarly colored flowers in a much smaller size

Samson

Bred as a show chrysanthemum, Samson is a good example of a flower with a reflexed form, where all the all the petal tips point towards the floor.

This gives the flower a tidy, swept-back appearance. The youngest, newest petals are bunched into a rusty gold topknot in the center of the bloom, and as the flower matures, they elongate into a handsome umbrella of deep red.

Samson is classed as an early-flowering chrysanthemum, arriving as autumn really starts to get into its stride. For show purposes, a polytunnel or greenhouse will preserve the perfection of the exhibition bloom, but the plant will also grow and blossom outside, producing sprays of flowers that can be cut for seasonal arrangements, and then lifted for winter protection.

Samson is classified as 2a or "Reflex" in the US, and 9c in the UK.

....

Flower type Exhibition and floristry
Flowering period Early autumn
Hardiness rating USDA Zone 9; RHS H3
Form Reflexed
Flower size Large
Color Rich, toasty red
How to use Arrange in an earthenware vase alongside grasses, seedheads and autumn leaves; stems can also be disbudded and used for exhibition
Alternative varieties Christopher Lawson and Bronze Matlock are similarly stunning early show varieties; mid-season Doreen Statham can be grown in a pot outside, then brought under cover to flower

PIP Salmon

The advantage of commercial cut flowers is that they are available over a long period, or even all year round. And although this has in recent history given chrysanthemums a reputation for being dull but bomb-proof, change is afoot with modern introductions such as PIP Salmon.

Its creamy apricot blooms have a deeper caramel stripe, and although they are produced with no particular restrictions on timing, they lend themselves particularly well to autumn. The lightly brushed streaks add detail without being fussy, and impart a gentle texture that helps the flower blend with other components of a bouquet.

The colors are subtle and sweet, and combined with cream or peach roses, apricot *Lisianthus* and dark-colored *Astrantia*, they would look lovely with a *café au lait* wedding dress. Alternatively, use in an urn or as a table arrangement with dark burgundy hydrangeas, wine-colored dahlias, rosehips and eucalyptus.

Flower type Commercially grown florists' variety
Flowering period Available all year round as a cut flower
Hardiness rating USDA Zone 9; RHS H3
Form Decorative
Flower size Medium
Color Soft apricot with coffee and damson
How to use The subtle colors work well with dried flowers and seedheads, and with bare twigs or sprays of autumn foliage
Alternative varieties Serenity Salmon is a commercial variety with similarly streaked centers and an Anemone form; for the garden, Picasso (see p.174) has small pink-terracotta flowers on a mounded plant

Peter Magnus

Bred by Ted King, of renowned nursery King's Mums in the US, Peter Magnus is a most charming chrysanthemum.

The flowers are produced liberally on fairly compact plants and they are a classic Anemone in form. A double frill of stubby, lavender-pink petals surrounds a hub of tightly packed disc florets, while a central dimple of ground coffee hue fades as the flower matures, until the tips are just brushed with ochre.

Peter Magnus is classified as 8c in the US and 12b in the UK, and alongside cultivars such as Rose Maiko and Bronze Fleece, it is a Cascade. Unlike some of the other exhibition forms, these require no stopping or pinching out. Cascades can be grown to create a waterfall of flowers or trained into sculptural forms, an art that has been perfected in Japan, although it has fallen out of fashion somewhat in the west.

For cut-flower purposes, Peter Magnus can be left to grow upright and sprays of blooms harvested as required.

....

Flower type Exhibition and floristry
Flowering period Mid- to late autumn
Hardiness rating USDA Zone 9; RHS H3
Form Anemone
Flower size Small
Color Baby pink with a hint of old gold
How to use Cut sprays to include in wedding or christening bouquets, grow in a container as a conservatory plant or experiment with training for a dramatic, if temporary, indoor display
Alternative varieties For the form, try Rose Maiko or Pink Fleece; commercial variety Jeanny Rosy (see p.106) is a pretty pink Pompon that gives a similar impression in an arrangement

Kalimba Rosy and Kalimba Salmon

Bred by Dekker Chrysanten in the Netherlands, the Kalimba Series is one of those increasingly numerous groups of modern all-purpose chrysanthemums that are versatile, highly adaptable and can be used in almost all floristry situations.

With cheerful colors combined with the daisy family's usual charming form, the Series has the work ethic of the very best chrysanthemums, succeeding effortlessly in single-variety arrangements and playing nicely with other flowers, too.

Kalimba Rosy and Kalimba Salmon (see p.242) are simply excellent flowers, and where pink is not the *couleur du jour* and something stronger is required, Kalimba Orange is also available.

Flower type Commercially grown florists' variety
Flowering period Available all year round as a cut flower
Hardiness rating USDA Zone 9; RHS H3
Form Decorative
Flower size Medium
Color Shell-pink or pale salmon
How to use Can be bought as sprays or disbudded single blooms and used in whatever way is required
Alternative varieties Other commercial blooms include Pastela Rosé and Baltica® Salmon

Carmine Blush

Cheerful, fizzy pink with magenta undertones, Carmine Blush is a Korean Group chrysanthemum that barrels onwards, regardless of the approach of winter.

When other plants have fallen or failed, its sweetly scented daisies provide color and energy in the autumn border, the paler pink blooms contrasting nicely with their darker buds and offering a supply of nectar for brave, late-flying insects.

The plant is compact with dense, well-divided foliage. Highly floriferous and impressively weatherproof, it earns a place in more exposed gardens, for example near the sea. It could also be used to provide autumn interest in other tricky-yet-sunny locations, such as balconies and roof gardens.

Selected by Bob Brown of Cotswold Garden Flowers in England, Carmine Blush gained a Royal Horticultural Society Award of Garden Merit in 2009 and is classified as 21d in the UK.

Flower type Hardy garden plant
Flowering period Late autumn to winter
Hardiness rating USDA Zones 7–9; RHS H5
Form Single
Flower size Small to medium
Color Light pink
How to use Pretty in a posy or buttonhole and weatherproof enough to make a good garden plant
Alternative varieties Selly Oak Purple has attractive single flowers and Clara Curtis does the same job in the garden, but starts two and a half months earlier

Breitner's Supreme

Daisies have recognizable consistency to them and, should Breitner's Supreme be viewed in a line-up of, say, little lawn daisies, glorious oxeye daisies, sharply pungent feverfew, leucanthemums, shasta daisies and marguerites, it quite clearly carries the flag of family resemblance with pride.

Rare in cultivation, the plant is fairly low-growing by garden chrysanthemum standards and it forms a loose, spreading mound of light green foliage which is topped with classically snowy daisies.

By the time the leaves are falling and the nights are drawing in, clean, clear white is a rare color in the garden and even among chrysanthemums, most flowers have a hint of mauve or a whisper of pink to moderate the boldness of their hue. But, perfect as a coat of fresh paint and bringing to mind a toothpaste commercial, Breitner's Supreme has a standout quality which means that its companions have to be carefully chosen.

This is not a plant that will sit well among the muted and golden hues of autumn, and dark colors are too great a contrast, but teamed with light blue salvias and pale pink asters or nestled up to the gray-green of a lavender hedge, harmony will be restored.

Flower type Hardy garden chrysanthemum
Flowering period Mid-autumn
Hardiness rating USDA Zones 8–9; RHS H4
Form Single
Flower size Medium
Color White with a green-gold center
How to use A garden plant; flowers can be cut for smaller posies
Alternative varieties White Gem and White Gloss have a similar color but different form, and both flower rather earlier; White Enbee Wedding is a taller single Spray chrysanthemum which might be a better choice for cutting but is less hardy

Beechcroft

With its spiced honey scent and large blooms in an elegant palette of biscuit, apricot and shell-pink, Beechcroft is the sort of fabulously classy flower that good florist–growers dream of at night, especially when they are planning for the wedding season.

In the garden it is tall and hardy, forming an upright plant around 36–45 inches tall and wide; it needs no staking and the leaves redden as the temperature drops in autumn. Old-rose and caramel buds open into uncharacteristically substantial flowers that fade decorously with age; the centers maturing from green to gold, which provides a beautiful gradation of color, together with beguiling depth and texture. The flowers may be single, semi-double and all stages in between on the same plant.

Sold by British chrysanthemum specialist, Halls of Heddon, in the 1970s, this is thought to be an old variety, but all records of its original provenance have been lost. It was therefore renamed by British plantswoman Rosy Hardy, who called it 'Beechcroft', for where it grew – in her mother's garden.

....

Flower type Hardy garden chrysanthemum
Flowering period Mid- to late autumn
Hardiness rating USDA Zones 7–9; RHS H5–6
Form Single or duplex
Flower size Medium to large
Color Sandstone to shell-pink
How to use Cut for wedding posies or to fill a vase; in the garden border, team with grasses and asters (*Symphotrichum*)
Alternative varieties Sheffield Pink; Sweetheart Pink has a similar coloring but a double flower

Icicles

Charismatic and beautiful, this chrysanthemum is supremely elegant. It is airy and pared back, and each floret has an intriguing twist to the end, while the color speaks volumes, being not merely and blankly snowy, but with the sea-green quality of compacted ice.

This chilly-sounding variety might seem a strange choice of wedding bloom, where the warmth of fond regard or the notional ideal of purity would surely be conceptually preferable to permafrost and ice queens. Yet the touch of redemptive color does wonders, lifting the temperature just enough that the flower can be teamed with pink asters or purple pompon dahlias, while petal-ends that are not so much hooked as notched or fringed, give the mature bloom a softness and charm.

The flowers are borne on a good, stocky plant with nice, dark green foliage. When disbudded they get substantial, but for floristry purposes they are better grown as a spray of blooms. Icicles is classified as 11a in the US.

Flower type Exhibition and floristry
Flowering period Mid- to late autumn
Hardiness rating USDA Zone 9; RHS H3
Form Spider
Flower size Medium to large
Color Greenish white
How to use For large, single Spiders, grow as a disbud, or cut sprays for looser bouquets, teamed with wax flowers, airy gypsophila and the earliest ranunculus, together with foliage such as eucalyptus or ferns
Alternative varieties Fantasy varieties include Mount Fuji and Chesapeake; for a commercially available cut flower, look for Anura Green, while for smaller, hardier "garden" varieties, check out Shaman's Vision or Korean Group chrysanthemum, White Gem

Dulwich Pink

Often listed in nursery catalogs as a Korean Chrysanthemum, Dulwich Pink was discovered – or rediscovered – in a garden in Dulwich Park in London, and since no records of its true identity exist, it was named for its location.

The daisy flowers are a lovely, warm pink color which lightens over time, while the bright gold boss of disc florets contrasts well with the darker, wine-pink buds. Arriving over several months from late summer to mid-autumn, depending on location, the weather-resistant sprays of blooms are produced liberally, and the plant is said to be tolerant down to −5.8°F (−21°C), although it is not keen on wet feet in winter.

Dulwich Pink received an Award of Garden Merit from the RHS in 2012.

Flower type Hardy garden chrysanthemum, 21d
Flowering period Mid-autumn
Hardiness rating USDA Zones 6–9; RHS H6
Form Duplex
Flower size Medium
Color Clear, bold pink
How to use Plant into autumn borders where the single flowers will provide a good nectar source for late-flying pollinators
Alternative varieties Alehmer Rote blooms about the same time and Mrs Jessie Cooper is reliably late-flowering – both are an attractive shade of fuchsia; American-bred Samba, meanwhile, has pale pink single flowers and blooms from late summer

EH Wilson

This classy little chrysanthemum takes its name from the British plant hunter and explorer Ernest Henry Wilson, who became known as "Chinese" Wilson due to his exploits in Asia. Over the course of his career, he introduced over 2000 plants to western cultivation, working first for the Veitch nursery in Britain and later for the Arnold Arboretum in Massachusetts, USA.

It is thought that this fine, airy, floriferous plant may in fact be a species chrysanthemum, introduced following one of Wilson's many trips during the first years of the twentieth century, and subsequently used for breeding.

With a profusion of small flowers, EH Wilson is rather charming. The fragrant, open, pale buttercream blooms are tiny, but their impact is boosted by a double layer of petals around a greenish-gold center, and they are carried on wiry, burgundy stems lightly frilled with small, grayish leaves.

In the garden, the plant will quickly form a spreading clump around 33–43 inches tall and 20 inches wide, which may benefit from staking. It works well alongside other small seasonal flowers such as asters, and it is popular with pollinating insects.

....

Flower type Hardy garden plant
Flowering period Late autumn
Hardiness rating USDA Zones 7–9; RHS H5
Form Single
Flower size Small
Color Pale cream
How to use Lovely when woven through a border; it cuts well and can be used as a filler in a mixed arrangement or as a seasonal buttonhole or corsage
Alternative varieties EH Wilson is unique among hardy garden chrysanthemums

Rosetta

Pretty as a picture and perfect either as a garden plant or cut for a vase, Rosetta was bred by French nurseryman Thierry Delabroye and is a worthy – and much hardier – alternative to pink pompon dahlias. Arriving appropriately early in the season and continuing until well into autumn, the flowers start off the sweet pink-orange of a summer dawn and open to paler pink, before fading almost to white.

The plant is sturdy and fairly compact, at around 20–28 inches high and 16 inches wide; it resents heavy soil and may benefit from being planted on a mound to improve drainage. To keep the display fresh, spent flowers should be removed regularly as they tend to go brown without dropping off.

It is worth noting that the name Rosetta is also used for a series of commercially grown florists' chrysanthemums in a range of colors including red and bronze, and the two should not be confused.

Flower type Hardy garden plant
Flowering period Late summer to mid-autumn
Hardiness rating USDA Zones 7–9; RHS H4–5
Form Pompon
Flower size Medium
Color Peachy pink and white
How to use A lovely cut flower, Rosetta would grace any wedding bouquet or table arrangement
Alternative varieties Pompon Girl, also raised by Thierry Delabroye, is similar; Mavis (AGM) is hardy, given dry feet, but the pink flowers are smaller; half-hardy Lavender Pixie can be grown in pots

Ruby Mound

One of the distinguished Mums from Minnesota™ (see p.20), Ruby Mound was raised by Dick Lehman of Minnesota, USA in the 1930s, and it is highly regarded amongst chrysanthemum aficionados.

The flowers are fluffy with a charmingly tousled bed-head quality and a delicate, classic chrysanthemum perfume, rather reminiscent of the soap you get in a superior, old-fashioned hotel. The color, too, is captivating; a rich and intense red with undertones of maroon, russet and dark chocolate, which remains steadfast with time.

The plant itself is 28–43 inches tall and 24 inches wide; starting off as a fairly tidy cushion, it gradually becomes more upright and lax, and increasingly benefits from staking. In the UK and other areas where winters tend to be wet, care should be taken over drainage and a protective mulch is advised.

Ruby Mound received an RHS Award of Garden Merit in 2005. It is classified as 21c in the UK and 4C in the US, and it is and assigned to the Korean Group.

Flower type Hardy to half-hardy garden plant
Flowering period Early to mid-autumn
Hardiness rating USDA Zones 8–9; RHS H3–4
Form Reflexed double
Flower size Small to medium
Color Rich, saturated red
How to use Perfect in a sunny, well-drained spot in the garden, it also cuts well for autumn arrangements
Alternative varieties The color is almost unique in the more hardy varieties, but half-hardy Myss Rihanna and Karen Taylor are good red Exhibition Sprays, while Bravo is a compact, rounded Cushion with a dark red flower

Mei-Kyō

Now a well-established and popular plant, Mei-Kyō arrived on British soil in the 1950s in a matchbox sent from Japan.

The fact that it makes complete sense that a novel and interesting plant should arrive romantically thus, speaks volumes about a social landscape shaped first by the stories of Christopher Robin and Pooh Bear, and later by those of the marmalade-munching Paddington Bear. And it also tells us a great deal about the world at the time. But so it appeared, shipped west by a friend to the care of nurseryman, alpine specialist and author, Will Ingwersen.

Often cited as meaning "Treasure of Kyoto," it is possible that where the plant is concerned, the name Mei-Kyō is actually more referential or conceptual in origin. For example, in Japanese a *meikyo* is a bridge with very special qualities, including a sense of harmony and balance, and several such bridges exist in the Kyoto prefecture. Alternatively, it may refer to clarity of mind and the essence of self-improvement – the "polished mirror" – which is linked with martial arts.

Forming a robust, fairly upright plant around 28 inches tall and 24 inches wide, the growing tips can be pinched out in midsummer to keep it bushy. Its small, dense, scented flowers shrug off rain and frost, and the plant tolerates winter wet.

Mei-Kyō has given rise to a number of notable and garden-worthy sports, including Nantyderry Sunshine and Bronze Elegance. It received an Award of Garden Merit from the Royal Horticultural Society in 2012 and is classified as 28b in the UK.

Flower type Hardy garden plant
Flowering period Late autumn
Hardiness rating USDA Zones 7–9; RHS H5
Form Semi-pompon
Flower size Small
Color Hot pink
How to use Creating a lovely splash of color in the autumn border or in a container, Mei-Kyō is also a very good cut flower
Alternative varieties Romantica is closest in form and color; Anastasia (not to be confused with Anastasia Green), Mavis (AGM) and Grandchild are a similar bright pink color but with larger flowers, while Purleigh White is identical in habit and form with delicious off-white flowers

Gold Laced

A charming and rather unusual chrysanthemum, Gold Laced was introduced by Eugen Schleipfer in 2015.

The double flowers are fairly small but they are striking. The scooped, almost boat-shaped petals are the color of caramel, with a gold picotee edge. This creates an attractive effect when the bloom is part-open, and the bunched florets in the center of the flower resemble a crown, or perhaps a brocade detail on a fine and courtly outfit.

In the border, generously proportioned Gold Laced makes a tall and substantial clump around 36–43 inches high and 43 inches wide, while its numerous buds look a bit like clouds of bright russet bumblebees hovering over the neat, dark, mauve-green foliage.

Although the individual flowers are bold, their small size stops them being too ostentatious and the plant is airy enough to fit into the autumn border alongside salvias, grasses and other seasonal flowers.

Flower type Hardy garden plant
Flowering period Early to late autumn
Hardiness rating USDA Zones 8–9; RHS H4
Form Double
Flower size Small
Color Burnt tangerine and old gold
How to use Unassumingly lovely in the border, or cut long stems to combine with autumn foliage in a large vase
Alternative varieties Granatapfel, also introduced by Schleipfer, has similarly two-toned flowers with pointed petals

Picasso

A compact, floriferous plant for the front of the border, Picasso is part of a series of chrysanthemums named for artists, with others including Cézanne, Rembrandt and Turner.

In the case of this artist, Picasso's claim to chrysanthemum fame is the still life of flowers in a vase, which he painted when he was 20 years old and which can now be seen in the Philadelphia Museum of Art. As can be seen from the painting, the loose, tousled stems of his inspiration are classic chrysanthemum style, but it is a very different look to the one that bears his name.

The eponymous plant is compact, dense and mounded. Healthy, dark green foliage is smothered in flowers that are about 1½ inches wide, and these are in a beguiling combination of rust, pecan and smoked salmon, offset by a speck of green in the center when the flowers are fully open.

Reliably out for Halloween in the northern hemisphere, Picasso creates a splash of seasonally appropriate pumpkin spice in the garden. It stands up well to heavy rain but is not completely hardy so it is worth giving it a bit of extra protection in winter.

Flower type Hardy to half-hardy garden plant
Flowering period Late autumn
Hardiness rating USDA Zone 9; RHS H3–4
Form Pompon
Flower size Small
Color Peach, soft cinnamon and toffee-gold
How to use A good plant for containers and smaller garden borders
Alternative varieties Bronze Elegance and Peterkin are similar, while Pennine Bullion is a much taller, half-hardy bronze Exhibition Spray chrysanthemum

Wild

Saffina Dark

Like a charmingly dishevelled floral hedgehog that has just arisen from its slumbers, Saffina Dark is a bold and confidently modern chrysanthemum, with a handsome halo of spiky quills.

Each thin, fine spine is a sophisticated honeyed caramel hue along its length, then tipped with gold and with rich purple-chestnut to the base. This combines to create a smoldering effect which is entirely appropriate to the season, echoing the way that the surrounding foliage changes, and colors gently mutate as days shorten and cool.

Its delightfully sunny alter ego, Saffina, has narrow golden petals which radiate from a terracotta heart, but while she is eminently worthy, the subtle, sultry qualities of Saffina Dark make it arguably more easy to use in arrangements.

Combine either or both in a vase with beech leaves, rust-colored fern foliage or dried grasses, and team with other chrysanthemums in dark red or dusty pink.

Saffina and Saffina Dark are classified as 10a in the US.

Flower type Commercially grown florists' variety, sometimes available for home growing
Flowering period Late autumn in the garden; available over a long period as a cut flower
Hardiness rating USDA Zone 9; RHS H3
Form Quill
Flower size Large
Color Bronze, burgundy and gold
How to use Pile into a vase for a long-lasting display
Alternative varieties Look for Baltazar Flame or Tula® Carmella; Buff Rayonnante has a similar form but in a peachy, *café au lait* hue

Senkyo Kenshin

While some Spider chrysanthemums are rather frail-seeming creatures, Senkyo Kenshin is different, with a mighty, almost chunky presence and a thundering form that in no way detracts from its prettiness.

When young, the flower sports a wiry central nest of green-gold, and although this is initially tightly packed, the tubular petals soon become too large to be contained. Creaking with slow-motion vegetable energy, they are gradually released, pinging out a few at a time to create a tousled forest of florets, each tipped with a neat curl.

Early in their journey, the still-developing flowers are an exciting and exotic addition to an autumn posy, contributing a frizzy, rather wild element to more static foliage displays and calmer blooms. But with maturity, order is restored and the composition becomes neat and expansive, at which point there is a sense of a completed performance as the flower goes "ta-dahhh!" and takes a bow.

Senkyo Kenshin is a Fantasy chrysanthemum, classified as 11a in the US and 10a in the UK. According to the British National Register, the color is officially Light Bronze, but in reality, it is far more than that, evolving and mutating in hue to take in tangerine, apricot, buttercup, toffee and pink.

....

Flower type Exhibition and floristry
Flowering period Mid- to late autumn
Hardiness rating USDA Zone 9; RHS H3
Form Spider
Flower size Large to very large
Color Bronze, peach and butterscotch
How to use A single spray in a vase is eye-catching and brings a bouquet to life; as a disbud, Senkyo Kenshin makes an excellent focal flower and it also lends itself to exhibition
Alternative varieties Goshu Penta, Symphony

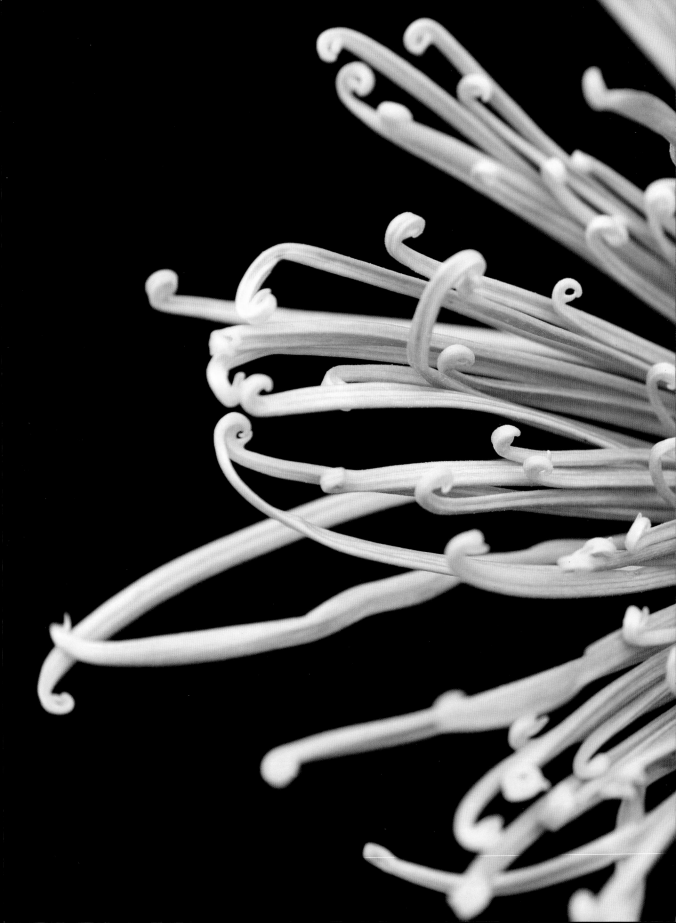

Etrusko

Not many flowers have a truly fluffy appearance, but densely double Etrusko bucks the trend.

The outer petals are a clear, bubble-gum pink with edges that appear frayed or snipped, and these are packed around a center that fades to a misty green – the pale pastel hue of lime and pistachio macarons – where the bloom has yet to mature.

Often sold as a disbudded single head, this is a good focal flower, and its size and vase-life, and all-round indestructible qualities, lend to its use at events and in decorations.

Fashionably new and intriguing, at first glance, Etrusko appears more like a cornflower or some other form of *Centaurea* than it does a chrysanthemum, but the pillowy blooms are curiously captivating, although they may yet divide opinion in some quarters.

Flower type Commercially grown florists' variety
Flowering period Available all year round as a cut flower
Hardiness rating USDA Zone 9; RHS H3
Form Dense double with fimbriated petals
Flower size Large
Color Very pink
How to use Use the cuddly, fluffy flowers of Etrusko and Etrusko White where their gentle softness will be appreciated, for example, in a christening bouquet or sympathy arrangement
Alternative varieties Etrusko White

Anastasia Green

Exotic and rather alien, the substantial spidery flowers of Anastasia Green are well known on the floristry circuit, where its vibrant double blooms bring an audacious chlorophyll zing and an element of surprise to arrangements.

As cut stems and as a potted plant, this variety is widely available, but in some places it is also possible to source rooted cuttings. These can be grown on at home, where they will form vigorous, upright plants with attractively lush foliage. Classed as half-hardy, the plant will carry on flowering well into autumn as long as it is in a very sheltered spot in the garden or under cover of glass.

Striking as a single-variety bouquet, Anastasia Green also works well as an accent flower. Its peculiar shade of lime-green combines with bright white to retina-searing effect, so it may be better to team it with green-whites and shades of purple for something more subtle and harmonious, or mix with bold pops of pink and orange for a contemporary combination of colors.

In the British National Register, the flower is classed as 10a/3 – a late-blooming Spider with a small flower; in the US it is 11B

. . . .

Flower type Commercially grown florists' variety and pot mum; sometimes available for home growing

Flowering period Mid- to late autumn as a garden plant; and widely available as a cut flower

Hardiness rating USDA Zone 9; RHS H3

Form Spider

Flower size Large

Color Arsenic green

How to use Widely available over a long period as a cut stem, Anastasia Green can also be grown under glass for late-season blooms on plants around 36in tall

Alternative varieties Shamrock Green or Green Mist, which flowers earlier and is more compact

Kokka Bunmi

Part of the excitement of chrysanthemums is their huge variety of form, and while some cultivars are modest little blooms and others justify their ubiquity through their sterling service, Kokka Bunmi is a drama queen of the highest order.

The flower is of a sort sometimes referred to in older books as a Japanese, or Japanese-style chrysanthemum, and these are really rather fabulous. Loosely incurved petals twist and snake in a glamorously dishevelled fashion, and lengthen to form a trailing curtain at the base of the flower as it expands and matures. The impact is further heightened by the two-tone coloring; each tubular floret is a hot, deep pink on the inside and a silvery blush color on the outer face, which gives the bloom even more character, if such a thing were possible.

Classified as 1a, or "Irregular Incurve" in the US, and Class 2 in the UK, Kokka Bunmi flowers relatively early for its group and the large plants are strong and healthy; this means that it can be grown outside in the back of the border, where it will flower until the frosts arrive. When disbudded, the blooms are magnificent, but they can also be left to grow as sprays of smaller blooms, which are a better fit for floristry or garden purposes.

Flower type Exhibition and floristry
Flowering period Mid-autumn
Hardiness rating USDA Zone 9; RHS H3
Form Incurved
Flower size Large to very large
Color Pale pink and deep rose
How to use While Kokka Bunmi holds its own as an exhibition bloom, for florist–growers and home gardeners it is an exciting addition to the chrysanthemum portfolio
Alternative varieties Jane Sharpe (see p.196) has a similar trailing form in a red-and-yellow colorway; Vienna Pink has tangled spiralling petals and can be bought as a cut flower

Jane Sharpe

A beautiful, large chrysanthemum in the loose and rather wayward Japanese style, Jane Sharpe is a bit of a florist's dream come true.

The palette is a seasonally perfect blend, with two-tone petals that are rich tangerine-cream brushed with crimson to one side, and the tawny hue of stewed plum to the other, and as the flower unfurls into elegant cascading curls beneath the bloom, the petals reflex and the dominant color switches.

Use in a pumpkin-spice-inspired arrangement with other orange, bronze and yellow chrysanthemums such as PIP Sunny and Saffina Dark (see p.178), and add in some dried grass stems, twigs and berries for structure and additional texture.

An Australian introduction, Jane Sharpe is classified in the US as 1A and is in Class 2 in the UK.

....

Flower type Exhibition and floristry
Flowering period Late autumn
Hardiness rating USDA Zone 9; RHS H3
Form Irregular Incurve in the US, Reflexed in the UK;
Flower size Large
Color Amber and russet
How to use A versatile cut flower when grown as a spray; the disbudded blooms are a fine focal point in an occasion arrangement and they perform well on the show bench
Alternative varieties Red Amethyst; Crimson Tide produces rusty red flowers on stocky plants

Burnt Orange

On first impressions, the tiny, spidery flowers of Burnt Orange look as if they would fly away with just a puff of wind, cartwheeling into the sky like sci-fi dandelion clocks. But their sturdiness and resilience confound expectation and they form tenacious clouds of blooms that stand up to wet weather and even to frosts, remaining resolute, hardy and strong to the end.

The small, dark bronze buds soon develop a whiskery, sea-anemone quality, the tentacles becoming tipped with gold as they start to flare outwards. When the flowers are fully open, the tubular petals form splayed stars the color of wet terracotta, each one with a flicker of yellow on its spatulate tip, as if it were bursting into flame.

With its faint fragrance of spiced plum, Burnt Orange makes a good and long-lasting cut flower, with blooms that are carried on airy stems, daintily frilled with sharply incised gray-green foliage.

Interesting rather than ostentatious, it comes into its own as the late-autumn border subsides. The plants are a good size, around 48–55 inches, and pinching out the growing tips or cutting back by a third to a half in early summer will keep the plant bushy and compact.

....

Flower type Hardy garden plant
Flowering period Late autumn
Hardiness rating USDA Zones 6–9; RHS H4
Form Quill
Flower size Medium
Color Caramel-orange and gold
How to use A few stems will be appreciated in a small vase on the desk or kitchen counter, and they are a fun addition to a posy, too
Alternative varieties Matchsticks is a flower with similarly quilled petals, but it is double and with yellow petals and red tips, so the colors are the other way around; Kellies Red Fan and Fire Wheel are greenhouse varieties bred in Australia

Anura Green syn. Basilio

Dainty, spidery and slightly surreal, this little chrysanthemum is a bit like the rehabilitated and socially acceptable form of the magnificent show blooms – monsters which are undeniably impressive in form and size, but are perhaps a little bit much for everyday use.

The two-tone flowers of Anura Green, however, are both compact and characterful, with enough presence to add depth and interest to an arrangement, but discreet enough not to dominate.

Combine with other chrysanthemums: Anastasia Green (see p.188) and little buttons of Code Green (see p.206) will riff off the virescent theme, while the starry flowers will pop with shades of purple. Alternatively, create a mixed bouquet with white or pink variations of gypsophila, wax flower, phlox and roses, depending on what is in season.

A commercially grown variety, this chrysanthemum has the full name of Santini AAA Anura Green.

....

Flower type Commercially grown florists' variety
Flowering period Available all year round as a cut flower
Hardiness rating USDA Zone 9; RHS H3
Form Spider
Flower size Medium
Color White and green
How to use Sprinkle prettily through posies
Alternative varieties Forms may vary, but other green-and-white chrysanthemums include commercial forms Zembla Lime, Alibaba and Maradona, while Vesuvio (see p.211) and Energy can be grown at home

Bolte

In chrysanthemums, breeding is everything, and as a commercially important cut flower across the globe, they always have to perform. Improvements are therefore continuous, and new forms and colors are constantly being introduced.

Recently arrived Bolte sports hot-pink petals with a contrasting white border, and while it is striking, it stops just short of brashness. The name honors luxury event designer Timo Bolte, who was thrilled by the plant's arrival on the scene, and celebrated in London with a characteristically glamorous fashion shoot.

Yet on a more practical note, Bolte is a flower that typifies the value of modern chrysanthemums in floristry. The flowers have always been worthy, but the newer varieties are exemplary in their vase-life and their resilience – key qualities in cut flowers. The color palette is sublime and subtle, and from florists to fashionistas, chrysanthemum credibility is soaring as these blooms once more become objects of lust and desire.

Flower type Commercially grown florists' variety
Flowering period Available all year round as a cut flower
Hardiness rating USDA Zone 9; RHS H3
Form Anemone
Flower size Medium
Color Pink and white
How to use Highly versatile, they can be thrown gaily into a vase or incorporated into a wedding posy and used as a bold pop of color in the bridesmaids' posies
Alternative varieties Doppia, All-in and Disco Club are strongly bicolored florists' blooms; hardy chrysanthemums tend not to be as striking but there are some two-tone varieties such as 'Will's Wonderful'

Code Green

Small-flowered spray chrysanthemums are ultimately adaptable and Code Green is very popular in floristry for its ability to add intensity and punctuation, which suits it for almost any task in hand.

Resembling smart green buttons, the flowers are carried several to an attractively structured stem. The color is dark enough to offset yellows nicely, rather than ramping up the citrus acidity, and it looks particularly good blended with autumnal hues of bronze, russet and purple.

Use as part of an autumn-wedding bouquet, with beech leaves, dahlias, asters and colored foliage, and continue the theme by using compact Code Green in the buttonholes or corsages, too. If somewhat modest in the company of louche and shaggy blooms, it is still an effective foil and can also be used to echo the contrasting green center of other, related, flowers such as bright white chrysanthemum Chic.

....

Flower type Commercially grown florists' variety
Flowering period Available all year round as a cut flower
Hardiness rating USDA Zone 9; RHS H3
Form Pompon
Flower size Small
Color Rich, intense green
How to use Plays well with almost anything
Alternative varieties Kermit, Yoko Ono, County Green

Yellow Bokaa

There has recently been an explosion of chrysanthemums that have a strong contrast between the petals and the central boss of disc florets, and one of the finest is Yellow Bokaa.

This is part of the Madiba® Series, a line of plants named by breeder Dekker Chrysanten in honor of Nelson Mandela, whose nickname was Madiba. The idea is that the flowers will emulate his colorful robes, innate approachability and easy manner. Bokaa, meanwhile, is a village in Botswana.

Highly bred and carefully chosen for maximum appeal, this is part of the varied Santini Series, with its full name being Santini Madiba® Yellow Bokaa. And with dense sprays of small flowers smiling upwards like clusters of miniature sunflowers, Yellow Bokaa is absolutely charming.

In the garden, such bold color juxtapositions are less common but there is still a treasure trove of hardy chrysanthemums with a cheerful disposition and sunny demeanor. For darker centers, Brown Eyes is yellow and burnt orange, and Mavis AGM is pink, but it is also worth looking at varieties such as Neue Kokarde, Ruby Raynor, Bright Eyes and Nantyderry Sunshine, all of which are easy to grow and make good cut flowers.

....

Flower type Commercially grown florists' variety
Flowering period Available all year round as a cut flower
Hardiness rating USDA Zone 9; RHS H3
Form Anemone
Flower size Very small
Color Butter yellow and burnt toast
How to use Thoroughly enjoyable as a single-variety bunch in a sturdy jug
Alternative varieties White chrysanthemum Sun Up is a similar form to Yellow Bokaa, and other florists' chrysanthemums with high-contrast flowers are legion

Vesuvio

Weird, wild and decidedly unusual even by the exotic standards of chrysanthemums, Vesuvio looks like a flower that was dreamed up by the creative team of a 1970s sci-fi movie after a few too many late-night sherbets.

The flowers start off as an eminently reasonable cluster of thin quills, but as they expand, they fade from cream to fresh white, and the anemone center slowly morphs into a fluffy spherical pincushion. As the flowers develop, the puffball of disc florets then pushes the outer rays into a wide ring, like the first distant view of an exploding star.

When grown in the garden or greenhouse, the somewhat slender plant will reach around 24–36 inches tall and the sprays of fairly small flowers can be harvested as required. Vesuvio is also available as commercially grown stems. In addition to the white flowers, there is a yellow form if you like your floral space monsters in a range of colorways.

Vesuvio is classified as 8c in the US and 9f in the UK. It is PBR registered.

....

Flower type Commercially grown florists' variety; occasionally available for exhibition and floristry purposes
Flowering period Mid- to late autumn
Hardiness rating USDA Zone 9; RHS H3
Form Quilled Anemone
Flower size Small
Color Delicate white with a touch of early sunshine
How to use Cut a few stems for a small vase or use with Spider and Quill chrysanthemums as a counterpoint to larger blooms
Alternative varieties Anura Green

GROWING AND CARE

GIVEN SUNSHINE AND WELL-DRAINED SOIL, CHRYSANTHEMUMS ARE
CHEERFUL, BIDDABLE CHARACTERS. THEY MAY DIFFER IN FORM AND
TOLERANCE TO COLD, BUT THIS IS PART OF THEIR CHARM AND INTEREST.
SPEND A LITTLE TIME GETTING TO KNOW THEM, UNDERSTAND THEIR
HARDINESS AND AIM TO PROVIDE THE ESSENTIALS — THEIR OTHER
REQUIREMENTS ARE FEW; AND AS GLORIOUS GARDEN PLANTS AND
FLAMBOYANT CUT FLOWERS, THE REWARDS ARE GREAT INDEED.

As long as their basic needs are met, chrysanthemums are fairly forgiving plants, but because they have been bred for different purposes, this is something that must be taken into consideration in a garden setting.

Chrysanthemum is an horticulturally established genus, and there is plenty of cultivation information around, but many of the available books and websites have been compiled with a focus on the half-hardy varieties and with the objective of exhibition at least partly in mind. When it comes to hardy chrysanthemums, meanwhile, there is a comparative lack of fuss and they are referred to much less frequently.

The distinctions between the two are also not always explicit. Half-hardy show blooms are often provided with precise and detailed information regarding their cultivation needs, and since the growing instructions for hardy chrysanthemums could be written on the back of a postage stamp, they have tended to be overlooked.

That the same name is used for two dynasties of plants, related but largely disconnected, is confusing in itself. And because cultivation instructions for one type of chrysanthemum may not suit another type particularly well, one size does not fit all.

With a revival of interest, however, has come a change in priorities. For florist–growers and newly inspired enthusiasts, unravelling this is an exciting voyage of discovery. Whether approached out of personal curiosity or professional ambition, there is an emphasis on getting to grips with planting and cultivating chrysanthemums, and exploring their myriad forms. The most important thing is to end up with a plant that thrives and with flowers to enjoy. Classification, stopping times and disbudding are very much of secondary interest, at least at the outset.

Chrysanthemums can be hardy, half-hardy and all stages in between, so an important first step is knowing what sort of plant you have got. Hardy varieties can be planted in any reasonable, well-drained soil in a sunny spot, and largely left to get on with it. Cultivars that are less hardy may need to be brought under cover over winter, particularly in the case of the glamorous, late-flowering forms.

The next things to consider are what sort of site is available and what conditions are on offer, along with what you want your chrysanthemum plants to do. All gardens have a different combination of factors influencing what can be successfully grown, and shelter, drainage and temperature can all vary substantially. There are also tricks that can be used to improve your chances of success. The protection of a warm wall might extend the season enough for late-bloomers to flower even without a greenhouse, for example, while a raised area can tilt the odds in favor of those varieties that like dry feet.

Aim to understand the environment in which you are operating and the needs of the plant, and choose the best options. Learning along the way and enlightened trial and error may be slow, but this is the best route to success.

Selecting varieties to grow at home

With bunches of chrysanthemums in the shops all year round, it is easy to become detached from the natural seasonality of this particular plant, so when it comes to growing them in the domestic garden, it is worth looking at how they tick.

Chrysanthemums are short-day plants (see p.24). This means that they are naturally stimulated to bloom as the hours of daylight decrease in the latter half of the year. In the UK, they are generally categorized as Early, Mid-season or Late; this is applied most frequently to half-hardy exhibition and floristry blooms. Early-flowering chrysanthemums bloom from late summer to mid-autumn, and often very much later as long as the weather stays mild; mid-season types flower until mid-autumn – although these can arrive surprisingly promptly as the seasons turn and should last until the frosts; while late-flowering chrysanthemums bloom

under cover from late autumn to mid-winter. In the US the same information is often conveyed by indicating a flowering window.

Within these categories, there is a wide range of terms and descriptions for the different classes and sub-classes of bloom. And it is easy for the uninitiated to come unstuck when faced with a bewildering array of Koreans, Rubellums and garden sprays, with "early" plants that are still in flower chronologically late in the year, "garden" varieties that need to be overwintered indoors and "greenhouse" varieties that can grow in pots outside until winter descends and are only then brought into the warm, in order to flower.

There are, however, a number of useful, if general, anchor points. Firstly, hardy garden chrysanthemums are just that: plants that thrive in the border like any other herbaceous perennial, assuming reasonable sun and drainage. In Britain, these are classified as section 21, where they are classified at all.

Secondly, although the words Korean and Rubellum are often bandied around, these are groups of hardy plants that originally arose in the 1920s and 1930s through American and British breeding programs respectively (see p.20). They are essentially brand names, therefore, and although the terms do convey some information about their specific heritage, they have been extensively interbred over the years to produce numerous vaguely related descendants.

Next, there is a fairly large gray area consisting of plants which will happily flower outside, but may need to be brought inside for winter as they are intolerant of cold, wet or both. There are also plants that are borderline-hardy or mostly half-hardy, but may get through winter outside if they are given protection in the form of a mulch or cover, or if they are on very well-drained soil in a sheltered location.

It is also worth knowing that all the really fancy flowers – the huge Spider types, the Quills, the ones with cascading tentacles and so on – are half-hardy. And not only do these flower late in the season, from late autumn to winter, they need greenhouse protection to do so. If that is what you want to grow, therefore, you will need to plan accordingly.

Although rather involved, the system of classification on pp.26–29 is a good way of understanding how a registered chrysanthemum will behave, when it will flower and broadly how it will look, and this can be used to further narrow down the options.

As a gardener, one has to take a view. Chrysanthemums are legion, so pick one that does the job required. If the aim is to deliver a nice splash of color in the herbaceous border, there is no point in choosing a diva that needs a greenhouse. And for sprays of late, cut flowers throughout the autumn, there will be a wide range of options available to suit your needs and site.

Making sensible decisions about what is practically possible will make for a far more rewarding gardening experience. Plants can be grown in pots for easy relocation and protection, or it may just be simpler to buy a hardier or earlier-flowering form that does the same sort of thing visually, and may be left to grow outside. Once plants are large enough to divide, there will also be scope for experimentation with particular cultivars, bringing some plants inside for security and leaving the others to battle the elements.

As discussed on p.11, it is a good idea not to get too hung up on particular varieties. Many thousands of cultivars are in circulation and more

HARDINESS

There are a range of charts and tables to indicate what level of chill a plant will tolerate. Two useful systems are produced by the United States Department of Agriculture (USDA) and the Royal Horticultural Society (RHS), which range from tropical to extremely hardy.

USDA
Zone 3: −40°F to −30°F (−40°C to −34°C)
Zone 4: −30°F to −20°F (−34°C to −29°C)
Zone 5: −20°F to −10°F (−29°C to −23°C)
Zone 6: −10°F to 0°F (−23°C to −18°C)
Zone 7: 0°F to 10°F (−18°C to −12°C)
Zone 8: 10°F to 20°F (−12°C to −7°C)
Zone 9: 20°F to 30°F (−7°C to −1°C)
Zone 10: 30°F to 40°F (−1°C to 4.5°C)

RHS
H3: to −5°C (23°F), half-hardy
H4: to −10°C (14°F), hardy in an average winter
H5: to −15°C (5°F), hardy in a cold winter
H6: to −20°C (−4°F), hardy in a very cold winter
H7: colder than −20°C (−4°F), very hardy

Because these systems do not equate exactly, the specified hardiness in the plant profiles in this book (pages 46–211) are an approximation, and local variations in climate will play a part. Nurseries will often indicate a lowest known temperature, particularly in the case of hardy plants.

are introduced each year, while others inevitably vanish. Flowers shared on social media may not always be locally available, so choose the best-fit alternative and carry on with gardening, arranging and showing what you have got.

Buying chrysanthemum plants

For simplicity, chrysanthemums bought for growing at home can be divided into three categories: hardy border chrysanthemums, pot mums and exhibition types.

Hardy chrysanthemums are garden plants and can be found in good nurseries alongside other herbaceous perennial stock. Pot mums, meanwhile, are compact containerized plants, widely available all year round to give an instant hit of color. The chrysanthemums that are equally well-suited to exhibition and floristry are half-hardy, and they are usually bought as plug plants or rooted cuttings.

When chrysanthemum shopping, aim to select plants that are as healthy and well-grown as possible. Pot mums should have foliage that is lush and green, with no signs of wilting or drought, and they should have plenty of flower buds waiting to bloom. Hardy varieties may not be ready to bloom, but even in winter there is often fresh growth in the top of the pot of a thriving plant, so choose the best specimen available. Check the leaves for spotting and discoloration, and steer away from plants that have moss growing on top of the pots or that have clearly been standing in water.

Speciality chrysanthemums for cutting and exhibition are becoming increasingly popular, so it is worth getting organized and ordering early for the best choice. Usually half-hardy, they can be shipped from mid-winter to late spring, and you can generally indicate your preferred delivery date when ordering, according to whether or not you have greenhouse space. Pot up immediately on arrival and protect from frost.

Nurseries can quickly sell out of their most desirable forms, or may restrict orders to one plant of each variety. But once acquired, chrysanthemums are easy to propagate (see pp.232–233), which will rapidly increase your stock of favorites.

Growing chrysanthemums

Chrysanthemums are happiest when grown in a warm and sheltered location, with plenty of sun and soil that is fertile and free-draining. Some shade can be tolerated, but they won't do well in heavy or wet conditions. In particular, soil that becomes waterlogged in winter is likely to be the end of them.

As discussed on pp.220–222, hardiness varies. Some border chrysanthemums can tolerate temperatures of –6°F (–21°C) although not all are quite this robust; others have distinctive foibles, such as the original Korean varieties, which were bred for chilly Connecticut but which dislike wet feet. Likewise, the Mums from Minnesota are not too concerned by cold but damp soil is a different story. The cultivars most prized for floristry and exhibition, meanwhile, are almost exclusively half-hardy plants, and although some may flower in the garden, they are usually best overwintered indoors.

Garden plants

When planting outdoors, pick a site that gets at least six hours of bright sunshine a day, and bear in mind that a spot that is sunny in summer may become more shaded later. It is best to avoid planting chrysanthemums next to a bright outdoor light, which might artificially extend day length and inhibit flowering (see p.24).

POT MUMS

Available in every supermarket and garden center, pot mums are floriferous dwarf chrysanthemums which lend themselves to gifting and a range of ornamental uses. Often treated as disposable or considered to be a short-term house plant, most pot mums are half-hardy perennials and can usually be managed like others of their kind – either grown outside in summer and overwintered indoors, or planted in a sheltered, well-drained location and left to take their chances.

Historically, pot mums were treated with a dwarfing hormone that reduced the stem length between the nodes to keep them compact. If they were then planted out, the hormone would gradually wear off, resulting in much taller plants the following year. More recently, however, directed breeding has resulted in naturally dwarf varieties.

Improve soil as necessary by adding organic matter, then plant as usual and water well. On heavy ground or in wetter areas, it can be worth creating a small mound, say 4–6 inches higher than the surrounding soil, and planting the chrysanthemum on top for extra drainage. On clay soils, mounds slump back fast, but a heap of sand will last longer, or consider building a raised bed.

Half-hardy plants can flower outdoors until late autumn in a sheltered, south-facing garden, particularly if a slope provides drainage. Unless the climate is very favorable, however, the plants are usually best lifted to overwinter indoors. The late autumn- and winter-flowering cultivars, meanwhile, are best grown in a greenhouse, or in containers that can be moved inside as winter approaches.

Growing under cover

For showing and floristry, perfection is easier to achieve with a greenhouse or polytunnel for protection. If your covered area has soil borders and plenty of space, rooted cuttings can be planted out when they arrive in spring. These should be spaced so that there is approximately 16 inches between plants, and thoroughly watered in.

Alternatively, use large pots with one chrysanthemum cutting to each 5–6 gallon (13–14 inch) container (see below). In this way, even the "lates" can be brought on outside in summer, leaving room for other glasshouse crops in the interim.

In both cases, best results will be achieved by staking the plants, and with regular feeding and watering.

Growing in pots

As pot mums, chrysanthemums are famous container specimens, and whether hardy or half-hardy, floriferous hummocks or compact-but-upright in form, the options are extensive.

Delicate and weather-sensitive "lates" particularly lend themselves to this. Because they can live outside in summer and then be brought indoors to flower, they are frequently pot-grown for convenience.

Fill containers with a good-quality, peat-free potting compost; this should be free-draining but moisture-retentive and reasonably nutritious. A good general-purpose potting compost should be fine, or you can formulate your own. Websites and books aimed at growing for shows offer specific advice on this area.

Hardy plants can live outside just like any other container perennial, while half-hardy specimens, including those sold as pot mums, can be put outside in the garden once there is no further risk of frost. Depending on variety and how mature the plant was at point of purchase, they can flower from midsummer through until late autumn or early winter if they are regularly fed and watered. Repot every two years or so, or as necessary to keep the plant growing well.

Once the weather starts to cool, bring the pots under cover or insulate them with sacking to keep them frost-free and fairly dry until spring.

Care and maintenance

The amount of care and maintenance that chrysanthemums need depends heavily on what they are grown for. Plants destined for exhibition or floristry will require a robust feeding and watering regime to support show-bench perfection or a high degree of productivity. Hardy plants require less input, but they can still benefit from a little attention at the right time.

Feeding and watering

Chrysanthemums are not hugely hungry plants and if they are grown outside in decent soil with organic matter added on planting, they are relatively low-maintenance. A mulch once or twice a year will help to keep the soil in good condition, and on poor ground, a boost with general-purpose feed or seaweed tonic in early summer can be helpful. In periods of dry weather, water deeply every few days, or as necessary.

When the plants are grown in containers, the compost should be kept moist but not soggy, and a balanced liquid feed applied fortnightly during the growing season until the flowering buds appear. The same rule applies for chrysanthemums planted into a greenhouse border.

Chrysanthemums dislike too much water and they actively dislike winter wet, but they are not completely immune to drought, either. If they are growing in a container in a sunny spot, the soil can dry out very quickly and they may wilt. As the plant outgrows its root-room, repot into a larger container.

Managing the plant

While many hardy chrysanthemums and pot mums don't need any particular management, some will benefit from deadheading or a late-spring cut-back to keep them tidy and compact. For the purposes of floristry and the show bench, however, persuading the plant to perform in a particular way is essential to success.

Deadheading Tired flowers and dead leaves can be removed for aesthetic purposes, using clean secateurs or a sharp pair of scissors. This may also help prolong the show, but in the case of most hardy chrysanthemums, it is not strictly necessary.

Pinching out This is where the tips of the shoots are removed in late spring or summer in order to create a bushier plant with more flower-bearing side shoots, or to manage form. To create sprays of show blooms, the leading or apical shoot of the main stem is removed, which allows the lateral buds to develop; sometimes these are then also removed to create a second "crown" of flowers (see opposite).

For flower-growers, the ideal is a nice sturdy plant which will produce lots of material for picking, so pinch out the tips when plants get to approximately 6–8 inches high, retaining the bottom three or four leaves. Hardy garden chrysanthemums don't generally need pinching out, but if it is a tall variety and the location is exposed, cutting back plants by a third to a half in early to midsummer can keep them bushy and compact, and produce more flowering stems.

Disbudding This is a process used to produce a single magnificent flower on the top of each stem – perfect for floristry or showing. As the plant starts into growth in spring, remove surplus shoots so you end up with 2–4 stems. As these extend, continue to pinch off the side shoots in the leaf axils.

With no lateral flowers waiting in the wings, a cluster of buds will appear at the top of the stem. Choose the best one to keep, which is usually the apical bud, and remove the rest over a period of several days or a week. This single, solitary flower bud will then receive all the plant's energy, so when it blooms it will be as big as possible.

Staking

Not all chrysanthemums require staking; it depends on the variety and their purpose.

With hardy garden chrysanthemums, simply consider the plant, assess the site and take a view. Short, sturdy plants will need no staking, while medium-sized ones may get away without it when grown in a sheltered spot or if supported

STOPPING

Stopping is a technique that helps control at what point chrysanthemums flower, and it is used when growing plants for a particular show or event. Pinching out the tip in "earlies" – the plants that flower in early autumn – encourages production of sideshoots sooner than would otherwise be the case, hence earlier flowering.

In late-flowering varieties, the flowers can be delayed by stopping the plant once or twice, allowing it extra time to grow strong and enabling better-quality blooms.

When growing purely for pleasure, stopping is unnecessary as the plant will create what is termed a "natural break," where sideshoots arrive in due course and flowers are produced over a period of several months.

Suppliers will often indicate stopping dates in their catalogue, but it is worth remembering that these vary according to cultivar and latitude, so should only be used as a guideline.

by surrounding plants. On a windy site or in an exposed location, the lankier cultivars may need a hoop support or circular frame, or they can be braced using a discreet framework of pea sticks constructed early in the season.

Plants with long stems that are being grown for cutting or for exhibition will usually need to be staked on planting, using one vertical cane per stem. Tie in with soft twine to make sure they are straight and well supported. Single disbud chrysanthemums should be tied in regularly all the way up to the bloom – this is particularly important with show chrysanthemums – while sprays only need to have the main stem supported.

Overwintering

Once the flowering season is over, hardy garden plants can be allowed to die back naturally. The standing stems will provide winter structure and hibernation spaces for wildlife, and help protect the crown of the plant from frost. A thick mulch will protect the soil, helping to improve structure and water retention and also insulating the dormant crown and surface roots

Growing conditions vary, as does the hardiness of individual cultivars. If a hard frost is forecast or the location is particularly chilly, covering borderline-hardy specimens with a layer of sacking or an old blanket is advisable. Take insurance cuttings as necessary.

Where chrysanthemums are not hardy, overwinter in an unheated greenhouse or shed. Lift garden plants, and carry container-grown plants and pot mums indoors. Keep sparingly moist until the arrival of new growth in spring.

Propagation

There is something very satisfying about multiplying a favorite plant, and since the best cut flowers come from young, fresh plants, maintaining a constant supply of these is a good idea. Certain modern introductions have a PBR designation, a kind of horticultural copyright or patent where plant breeders' rights are protected; for onward sale, these can only be propagated under license, but there are many established and heirloom plants to which this does not apply.

Taking cuttings

Cuttings are preferably taken in spring, as the plants start to produce fresh growth, and later in the season, pinched-out shoot tips can be rooted as well. Cut off a section of basal shoot about 8cm (3in) long. Remove the lower leaves, trim the base of the stem to a node, then plunge into a pot of gritty multi-purpose compost and water well. A medium-sized pot will take around half a dozen well-spaced cuttings. Put this in a warm, bright place out of direct sunlight, and maintain a humid environment using a propagator or reusing a clear plastic bag. Later in the season, pinched-out shoot tips can be rooted as well.

Roots should start to appear within a few weeks. When there are signs of new growth, the young plants can be potted up and kept in a frost-free place until spring. Protect from full sun until the plant has been hardened off.

Another, quicker, way of getting a rooted cutting is to let the plant do the work for you. As the stool comes into growth, new shoots often emerge around the periphery of the main plant. Digging down will reveal that each shoot already has its own roots; sever from the parent plant with a sharp knife, then pot up and grow on.

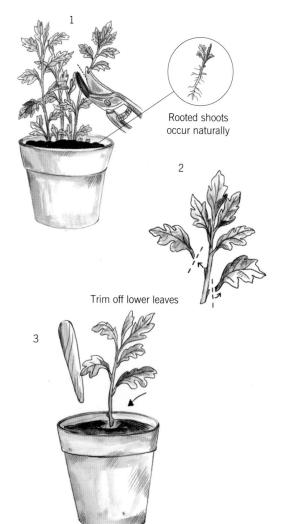

Rooted shoots occur naturally

Trim off lower leaves

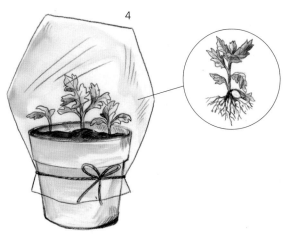

When taking cuttings from multiple specimens, always clean your tools between plants to guard against disease – most growers use a squirt of bleach or pass the blade through a lighter flame to sear the surface, although horticultural disinfectants are available.

Remove plant

Divide plant

Repot

Dividing plants

Mature stools and plants that have outgrown their pots can be divided in spring. This provides new individuals and also reinvigorates clumps which have become tired and overgrown.

Knock the plant out of its pot or dig up the root ball; remove any loose earth then divide into sections vertically. This can be done using an old bread knife or a trowel, or by hand if the specimen is small enough. Replant the sections in the garden or into their own pots, and give any surplus plants to chrysanthemum-loving friends and neighbors.

Growing from seed

Many chrysanthemums are fertile but they don't come true from seed, so specific varieties will need to be propagated through division or by taking cuttings. For something new and unique, however, sowing seeds is a voyage of discovery.

Mixed packets of seeds are commercially available, or as flowers fade, ripe seeds can be collected, dried and stored in a cool place until you are ready to start sowing. In late spring, sow the seeds thinly and evenly into a tray of fine compost; cover with a little more compost and water from the bottom. Take care not to overwater subsequently.

Best results will be achieved, particularly with the half-hardy varieties, by starting them off in a greenhouse or on a warm windowsill, out of direct sunlight. Cover with a propagator, an old, clear polythene bag or a piece of glass to keep the air humid. When the seedlings are large enough to handle, prick them out into individual pots of compost and grow on until they are ready to plant out in the garden or greenhouse border.

GROWING FOR SHOWS

Chrysanthemum has been grown for shows over a very long period (see pp.14–20) and many of the idiosyncrasies pertaining to its classification and cultivation have been driven by the desire to produce flowers that are in tip-top condition and are the archetype of their kind.

Growing plants for exhibition and competing against peers and experts can be addictive once you've got the bug. Sadly, the activity of showing chrysanthemums has declined in the last three or four decades but a renewed interest in the garden forms and a boom in artistic floristry may reverse this. In the meantime, the old hands at local and regional chrysanthemum shows may give no quarter in combat but they will certainly welcome fresh blood and new and interested faces, and may even list amateur categories to give first-time entrants a taste of the fun.

Start with research: study catalogs, work out what are considered to be the best-performing cultivars, their specific classifications and groups, and their desirable qualities. Visit a number of shows to size up the competition and get a feel for the staging process. Your nearest chrysanthemum society will be able to offer advice and encouragement.

Give yourself every advantage you can. Take time to practice the art of growing the perfect chrysanthemum, with all the staking and feeding, stopping and pinching out that that entails and choose cultivars that flower in the conditions available. For example, if you have no greenhouse, early disbuds and sprays are a better choice than lates, while smaller flowers tend to be less more weather-sensitive. Protecting the plants by building a shelter or windbreak can make all the difference when it counts.

On the show bench, perfection and poise is all. Blooms should be at their absolute peak, sprays should be well balanced and groups of flowers should be identical. Flowers are usually groomed so no petal is out of place, and the finer points of titivation are minute and absorbing.

Successful cultivation and staging is, therefore, a technical and extremely skilled process. The scope of this book does not permit its in-depth discussion, but existing literature on the subject is extensive. Established specialists, such as Halls of Heddon in the UK, have informative website. See p.42 for other societies and key contacts.

Pests and diseases

Chrysanthemums are usually healthy plants, and as long as they are not over-watered and get enough sun, they should be strong and fairly trouble-free. Plants that are in good condition are more resilient in the face of any potential challenges, so invest in good-quality specimens, grow them well and deal promptly with any issues that may arise.

With collections there is always potential for trouble to arrive with new acquisitions, so use a reliable supplier. Growing garden chrysanthemums in a mixed border physically separates the plants as well as encouraging a healthy ecosystem with plenty of predators to deal with any pests. Plants under cover are less vulnerable if the greenhouse or polytunnel is kept clean and tidy and they are not overcrowded.

Exhibition blooms will clearly require far more vigilance and primping than ordinary garden plants, and florists' chrysanthemums may benefit from protection, but if you are growing for pleasure and any damage or nibbling is purely cosmetic, there is no major cause for concern.

Pests

It is a universal law of gardening that the more cherished and expensive the plant, the more likely it is that something will want to eat it. Chrysanthemums are not overly troubled by pests, however, and in most cases, prompt action, reasonable tidiness and a certain amount of tolerance towards the other living things are all that are required. It is preferable not to use sprays and insecticides, even those that are organic or home-made, as they tend to have far-reaching destructive effects on organisms other than their target.

Caterpillars
A range of caterpillar species will eat chrysanthemums, particularly when these are grown in greenhouse conditions and natural predators have been excluded. Where visible damage can't be attributed to other culprits, such as earwigs and slugs, search among the flower petals or shake the stem to see if any caterpillars drop out. Picking them off by hand and, preferably, relocating to a less-prized plant, is usually sufficient.

Eelworms
A particular problem in persistently damp soil or where there is an overhead watering system, these are microscopic nematodes that feed on leaf tissue, which starts to turn black, starting at the bottom of the plant. Discard affected plants or treat with hot water (see p.237).

The pest can persist in the soil for some time, so don't plant chrysanthemums in the same place for several years after an infestation. When cutting or dividing, clean tools between plants (see p.233) to reduce the chance of transmission.

Slugs and snails
Given half a chance, slugs and snails will eat almost anything, and chrysanthemums are no exception. Growing in just-moist soil in full sun, a healthy plant will be resilient, but damp or shaded conditions can spell trouble. Even on established stools, new shoots can be grazed

back completely in spring, while cuttings and young plants are particularly vulnerable.

Even ravenous molluscs are part of the ecosystem, however, and rather than poisoning them it is better to manage the space so that the plants are a less easy target. Putting young potted plants and shooting stools onto a table until large enough to withstand grazing can help a lot.

Plants in the ground, meanwhile, should be sited in an optimum spot, and birds, beetles and other predators encouraged. Clear around the chrysanthemums early in the season to let air and light in, and reduce cover for slugs, who may turn their attention to easier targets.

Aphids and capsid bugs

Greenfly and blackfly are a perennial issue in gardens, and colonies can accumulate very rapidly. Large numbers of sap-sucking insects may weaken the plant, potentially spreading viruses, while their sticky honeydew can encourage sooty molds.

If the situation becomes critical, the bugs can be removed by squashing them or blasting them off the plant with a jet of water; this is preferable to using untargeted chemical sprays of any kind. If possible, just be patient; aphids are near the bottom of the food chain and are an important

source of nutrition for birds, ladybirds and a range of other small carnivorous beasts, and they will come and sort out the problem in due course.

Earwigs

Unappreciated even by the standards of the insect world, earwigs contribute to the garden clean-up team by eating detritus and small creatures such as aphids, but their habit of nibbling at the florets of dahlias and chrysanthemums has given them a bad reputation.

They are essentially friends with poor manners, however, so avoid putting chrysanthemums near heaps of leaves and cracks in masonry, where the nocturnal earwigs can shelter. Alternatively, find the insects somewhere else to hide, by stuffing an upturned flowerpot with straw or deploying rolls of corrugated card among the blooms. Once captured, the earwigs can be relocated elsewhere the following day.

Red spider mite

Usually associated with indoor or greenhouse plants, or with protracted periods of dry weather, red spider mite is a minute brown insect that is barely visible to the naked eye. Forming large colonies and creating fine webs on the underside of leaves, they can be hard to spot until the plants

HOT WATER TREATMENT

With care, certain pests and diseases, such as eelworms and white rust, can be eradicated by treating the plant with hot water. Lift the affected stool, trim the roots and cut back the remaining foliage before immersing the whole plant in a water bath that is held at 115°F (46°C). After five minutes, transfer the stools to a bath of cold water, then drain and dry in a well-ventilated place.

This process brings the temperature of the plant tissue up to the upper tolerance of most living things, but the application of heat needs to be quite precise – boiling the plant will kill it, but if the water is too cool, the procedure won't work.

start to suffer and the foliage becomes mottled and sickly.

Spider mite can be hard to get rid of, so prevention is better than cure, but if there is an infestation, remove the worst-affected leaves by hand and dispose of them. The mites are so tiny that they struggle to move in damp conditions, so mist the plants regularly to increase humidity and give them the nutrients they need to recover.

Vine weevil

Not usually a problem in open soil, vine weevils may be an issue in container-grown plants.

The adults are innocent-looking gray-black beetles, and while they may cause some leaf damage, this is minor compared to the destructive habits of their larvae. These C-shaped grubs with brown heads have a large appetite for succulents, heucheras and dahlias, and they are happy to tuck into chrysanthemums, too.

Where plants that were doing well suddenly stop dead and look sick, check for vine weevil larvae. Tip the plant out of its pot to inspect the roots – if there are any left. If larvae are present, throw the compost away, dispose of the larvae (fish or birds will be grateful) and repot the chrysanthemum into fresh compost. Leave the plant in light shade and don't overwater, and hopefully it will recover.

Vine weevil can be controlled by special, very specific nematodes. Order these online and water them into the compost once temperatures have increased in spring, and again in autumn, when the plants are still in growth.

Diseases

Good cultivation practices are useful in keeping many diseases at bay, and well-nourished, well-ventilated plants will be more resilient than those growing in adverse conditions. Aim to avoid infection in the first place by quarantining new arrivals and inspecting them regularly to make sure they are not bringing any problems with them. Remove any infected plant material promptly, clean tools assiduously, and don't take cuttings from diseased plants.

Rust

Usually appearing in late summer or autumn, there are two types of rust that afflict chrysanthemums, and the scale of the problem depends on which one presents itself.

Caused by the fungus *Puccinia chrysanthemi*, brown rust is the least damaging of the two. Pale green spots appear on the top of the leaf, with

dark brown pustules or concentric rings of affected tissue on the underside. It is less common in garden plants and can usually be controlled by picking off the worst-affected leaves, while good hygiene and a tidy greenhouse will help keep it under control indoors.

White rust, meanwhile, is caused by the closely related *Puccinia horiana* and it is far more of an issue, although susceptibility varies between cultivars. Pale spots on the top of the leaf become sunken and pinkish, or light brown pustules may develop on the underside; the leaves shrivel and the plant loses vigor.

Badly affected plants should be disposed of by burning or burying in a hole at least 12 inches deep. There are no fungicides licensed for use by the home gardener, but as a chemical-free alternative, treat the plants with hot water (see p.237), which also helps to control eelworm.

Powdery mildew

This often appears when the soil is too dry, as a dusting of gray or white on the leaves. Cut off the worst-affected foliage and water the plant well, submerging containerized plants in a bucket until the pot sinks and then leaving it to drain.

Misting to increase humidity can help, as can improving growing conditions.

Molds and rots

Various fungal infections affect chrysanthemums. Botrytis or gray mold is fairly common and there is a range of non-specific rots, too.

Botrytis appears on plant tissues as wet brown spots, which develop into the classic moldy filaments. It is a particular problem in greenhouses that are poorly ventilated, overcrowded, damp and cool. Carefully remove affected material to minimize the spreading of spores; watering should be reduced and ventilation increased.

Fungal rots thrive in wet weather and damp conditions. If the leaves start to yellow and the plant looks sick, or obvious black patches appear, then wet ground is likely to be implicated. Move potted plants to a drier area, such as next to a wall or into a greenhouse, and consider relocating garden plants to a better-drained location.

Viruses

Streaked, blotched or distorted foliage may be caused by any one of a number of viruses; these may be unsightly but they are not usually fatal. If the plant is badly affected or gives cause for concern, dispose of it by burning or burying at least 12 inches deep in a part of the garden where chrysanthemums don't grow.

GLOSSARY

AGM (Award of Garden Merit) Award given by the Royal Horticultural Society, which indicates that the plant is recommended by the Society and will perform well in the garden.

Anther The pollen sac at the end of the stamen.

Apical bud, apical shoot The main bud or flower on top of the stem, from "apex" meaning the highest part of something.

Basal shoot A shoot or new stem arising from the base of a perennial (or other plant). Fresh and fast-growing, they are good for taking cuttings.

Cultivar A cultivated form of the plant selected for its desirable characteristics.

Deadheading Removing spent flowers from the plant to encourage more blooms.

Disbud, disbudding Disbudding is the process of removing the lateral buds as a stem grows, to create a single large bloom. This is often referred to as a disbud.

Disc florets Small tubular flowers that make up the central disc in chrysanthemums, dahlias and other plants in the Asteraceae.

Duplex A flower with two layers of ray florets around a central hub of disc florets.

Fantasy (of chrysanthemums) A term used to collectively describe Quills, Spoons and Spiders.

Fimbriated The term used for the feathered or fringed effect at the end of the petals in some chrysanthemum cultivars.

Floret A single small flower that makes up part of a larger flower.

Hybrid A genetic cross between two different species, genera or cultivars.

Kiku Japanese word for chrysanthemum.

Laciniated See Fimbriated.

Node The point on the stem where a leaf emerges, often visible as a slight swelling or bump.

Open pollination Uncontrolled pollination between similar plants in the garden or field, where the offspring may differ from the parent due to the introduction of new genes.

PBR designation Where a commercially bred plant is subject to Plant Breeders Rights, which is a kind horticultural copyright.

Pinching out The process of removing the growing tip of a stem, to stimulate branching which leads to a bushier plant.

Pinnatisect This is where leaves are divided into pinnate lobes but these are not completely separate, and the leaf structures remain partially connected.

Polyploidy Where an organism possesses more than two sets of chromosomes. This is common in plants, and where the chromosome numbers between individuals are different, they may be incompatible and fail to hybridize.

Ray floret A small strap-shaped flower that, together with a number of others, forms the ray around the central disc in blooms in the Asteraceae family.

Species A population of individuals which have a high level of genetic similarity and which can interbreed.

Spatulate Where something is flattened at the end, like a spatula.

Sport A spontaneously arising mutation in part of a plant which can then be reproduced vegetatively as a new cultivar.

Spray A flowering stem where many small, or fairly small, lateral flowers are allowed to develop.

Stamen The pollen-producing (male) reproductive organ of a flower. It consists of a filament and anther.

Stool A term used to describe a perennial plant that has been cut down to the ground and from which new shoots will arise.

Variety A classification of cultivated plants, below subspecies, where minor but distinctive and inheritable characteristics are exhibited.

Vegetative propagation The process by which plants produce genetically identical new individuals, or clones.

INDEX

AUTHOR'S ACKNOWLEDGMENTS

This book is dedicated to Marilyn, my own mum, with love.

Writing a monograph inevitably requires a botanical deep dive, and with the twists and turns of research there will always be surprises. With a long tradition of cultivation resulting in divergent dynasties, and buffeted by the tides of fashion, chrysanthemums were never going to be an entirely straightforward subject, but if you look past a recent period in the doldrums, these are flowers with a lot about them to love. And with a clear resurgence of interest it seemed timely to consider the cultivated plant as a whole group, rather than focus on a single, horticultural and aesthetic silo.

I love a challenge and a voyage of discovery, and while I will have always enjoyed the pretty and hardy chrysanthemums that I grew up with, this investigation of the wider genus has been rewarding and eye-opening, and will be a fruitful avenue of experimentation for many years to come.

I must thank my family, Chris and our children, for their love, support and unswerving tolerance of my plant obsession. I am particularly grateful to my daughter, Holly, whose input and expertise smoothed the path of floristry inspiration and provided good companions for chrysanthemums in bouquets.

I am very grateful to all those who answered questions, proof-read text and were so generous with their time and knowledge. Thanks to Andrew and Helen Ward at Norwell Nurseries, for their warm welcome and excellent coffee, to Judy Barker for letting us loose in her collection, to Roger Brownbridge who patiently unravelled the complexities of chrysanthemum classification for me and to Joe Sharman whose broad expertise helped me understand the modern history of the plant, and bridge the gap between home cultivation and commercial breeding. Appreciation must also go to Marten Wouda and his colleagues at Dekker Chrysanten, for fact-checking and tidbits of information.

The team at Pavilion and HarperCollins has been as wonderful as ever, thanks to Stephanie Milner, Kiron Gill, Alice Kennedy-Owen, Shamar Gunning and Lily Wilson once again. I must also recognize and thank Somang Lee for her beautiful illustrations and Hilary Mandleberg for her editorial touch.

Finally, it is a pleasure as always to work with my friend and co-creator Georgianna Lane. Her eye is exquisite, her attention to detail is second to none and her drive to create something truly beautiful is unstoppable. She's braved the flower markets of Paris and locations in Burgundy and the Loire, and approached the rainy nurseries of England and unseasonal frosts of Virginia with fortitude. The result is a book that is elegant, detailed and inspiring, and a tribute to her skill.

PHOTOGRAPHER'S ACKNOWLEDGMENTS

My appreciation and gratitude to the executives and staff at Pavilion and HarperCollins UK for continuing to believe in and champion this series, and to the individuals who shepherded this latest title into being, notably Stephanie Milner, Kiron Gill, Alice Kennedy-Owen, Shamar Gunning and Lily Wilson.

My co-author and creative partner, award-winning writer Naomi Slade, approached this considerable project with grace and determination, creating a definitive resource for this complex and vast subject. Her always formidable skill with words continues to elevate these volumes with her lyrical and distinctive style, making them a joy to read.

The images in this book were photographed in France, The Netherlands, the United Kingdom and several locations in the United States, with the gracious assistance of many individuals and entities: Laetitia Mayor of Floresie, floral designer extraordinaire and dear friend, sourced an abundance of luscious blooms to create stunning portraits and arrangements in her charming French country studio in Burgundy. My appreciation to Judy Barker, who welcomed us to her section of the UK National Hardy Mum collection, and to Andrew and Helen Ward at Norwell Nurseries, for a most enjoyable, informative and productive shoot. A huge thank you to Marten Wouda and his colleagues at Dekker Chrysanten for generously enabling my visit to their facility and allowing me to photograph the nearly-overwhelming array of brilliant flowers during their Chrysanthemum Valley show at Hensbroek, Netherlands.

This book would be far less comprehensive in scope, in beauty and in the joy of chrysanthemums without the enthusiastic contributions of the ladies of Harmony Harvest Farm in Virginia. Chris Auville and her daughters Jessica Hall and Stephanie Duncan have a passion and vision for heirloom mums which is inspiring and infectious. Thanks also to General Manager Elizabeth for ensuring that I had the desired blooms to photograph, and to Floral Designer Mackenzie for the gorgeous arrangement on pages 44–45.

Un grand merci to the directors of the Conservatoire National du Chrysanthème Paul Lemaire in Ville de Saint-Jean de Braye near Orléans, France, for welcoming me to photograph this extensive and important heritage collection. My local florist in Paris, Les Fleurs de Sanji, provided the prettiest and freshest varieties available throughout the season. Thank you to Martin Hughes-Jones/Alamy Stock Photo for the use of the image on Page 71.

As always, I cherish and appreciate the ongoing support of my family in my global pursuit of capturing and chronicling the exquisite beauty of flowers.

10 9 8 7 6 5 4 3 2 1

Published in the United States of America by
Gibbs Smith
570 North Sportsplex Dr
Kaysville, UT 84037

Text © 2024 Naomi Slade
Photography © 2024 Georgianna Lane

Naomi Slade asserts the moral
right to be identified as the author
of this work

Library of Congress Control Number: 2024930631
ISBN: 978-1-4236-6561-8

First published in Great Britain by Pavilion,
An imprint of HarperCollins*Publishers* 2024

Printed and bound in China

This book contains FSC™ certified paper
and other controlled sources to ensure
responsible forest management.

FSC
www.fsc.org

MIX
Paper | Supporting
responsible forestry
FSC™ C007454

Throughout this book, every attempt has been made to refer
to each chrysanthemum variety by its most accurate and
appropriate name, bearing in mind breeding, registration and
commercial matters, but with ease of reading in mind. Should
any corrections be necessary, the publisher would be happy
to make them in any future printings.